AF740202

Tencent

In this book, author Min Tang examines the political economy of the China-based leading global Internet giant, Tencent. Tracing the historical context and shaping forces, the book illuminates Tencent's emergence as a joint creation of the Chinese state and transnational financial capital.

Tencent reveals interweaving axes of power on different levels, particularly interactions between the global digital industry and contemporary China. The expansion strategies Tencent has employed—horizontal and vertical integration, diversification and transnationalization—speak to the intrinsic trends of capitalist reproduction and the consistent features of the political economy of communications. The book also pinpoints two emerging and entangling trends—transnationalization and financialization—as unfolding trajectories of the global political economy.

Understanding Tencent's dynamics of growth helps to clarify the complex nature of China's contemporary transformation and the multifaceted characteristics of its increasingly globalized Internet industry. This short and highly topical research volume is perfect for students and scholars of global media; political economy; and Chinese business, media and communication, and society.

Min Tang is a lecturer in Media and Communication Studies and Global Studies at the School of Interdisciplinary Arts and Sciences, University of Washington Bothell. She holds a Ph.D. in communication from the University of Illinois at Urbana-Champaign. A critical political economy scholar, she studies how capitalist relations and power structures shape the provision system of communication and information in our society. Her current work examines information communication technologies (ICTs) as emerging sites of capitalist reproduction, with a focus on the Internet industry in China and the broadly defined Global South regions.

Global Media Giants
Series editors: Benjamin J. Birkinbine, Rodrigo Gomez and Janet Wasko

Since the second half of the 20th century, the significance of media corporate power has been increasing in different and complex ways around the world; the power of these companies in political, symbolic and economic terms has been a global issue and concern. In the 21st century, understanding media corporations is essential to understanding the political, economic and socio-cultural dimensions of our contemporary societies.

The **Global Media Giants** series will continue the work that began in the series editors' book *Global Media Giants*, providing detailed examinations of the largest and most powerful media corporations in the world.

Alphabet
The Becoming of Google
Micky Lee

Tencent
The Political Economy of China's Surging Internet Giant
Min Tang

For more information about this series, please visit: www.routledge.com/Global-Media-Giants/book-series/GMG

Tencent

The Political Economy of China's Surging Internet Giant

Min Tang

Routledge
Taylor & Francis Group
NEW YORK AND LONDON

First published 2020
by Routledge
52 Vanderbilt Avenue, New York, NY 10017

and by Routledge
2 Park Square, Milton Park, Abingdon, Oxon, OX14 4RN

Routledge is an imprint of the Taylor & Francis Group, an informa business

© 2020 Taylor & Francis

The right of Min Tang to be identified as author of this work has been asserted by her in accordance with sections 77 and 78 of the Copyright, Designs and Patents Act 1988.

All rights reserved. No part of this book may be reprinted or reproduced or utilised in any form or by any electronic, mechanical, or other means, now known or hereafter invented, including photocopying and recording, or in any information storage or retrieval system, without permission in writing from the publishers.

Trademark notice: Product or corporate names may be trademarks or registered trademarks, and are used only for identification and explanation without intent to infringe.

Library of Congress Cataloging-in-Publication Data
A catalog record for this book has been requested

ISBN: 978-0-367-19508-3 (hbk)
ISBN: 978-0-429-20289-6 (ebk)

Typeset in Times New Roman
by Apex CoVantage, LLC

To my mom and dad, Liu Huanxiu and Tang Xinfeng, whose aspirations and endeavors for a loving and beautiful world have made me who I am.

Contents

List of Abbreviations viii
List of Tables ix
List of Figures x
Acknowledgments xi

Introduction 1

1 History and Context 9

2 Economic Profile 32

3 Political Profile 62

4 Cultural Profile 83

Conclusion 108

Bibliography 114
Index 121

Abbreviations

CNNIC	China Internet Network Information Center
FDI	foreign direct investment
ICT	information and communication technology
IM	Instant Messaging
IPO	initial public offering
IVAS	Internet value-added service
MEI	Ministry of Electronics Industry
MIH	Myriad International Holdings
MII	Ministry of Information Industry
MIIT	Ministry of Industry and Information Technology
MMOG	Massive Multiplayer Online Game
MPT	Ministry of Posts and Telecommunications
MVAS	mobile and telecommunications value-added service
PCCW	Pacific Century CyberWorks
SEZ	special economic zone
VAS	value-added service
VC	venture capital
VIE	variable interest entity

Tables

1.1 Annual Gross Income in Chinese Telecom Industry 17
1.2 Annual Sales Income in Chinese Electronic Information Industry 17
1.3 Chinese Internet Companies Founded Between 1995 and 2000 21
2.1 Registered Capital of Original Shareholders 33
2.2 Tencent's Annual Balance, 2001–18 (RMB Million) 36
2.3 Tencent's Revenue by Business, 2001–11 37
2.4 Tencent's Revenue by Business, 2012–18 (USD in millions) 39
2.5 Research and Development Expenses, 2004–18 (RMB Million) 44
3.1 Tencent's Major Shareholders, 2004–18 69
3.2 Tencent's Board of Directors, 2004–18 70
4.1 Number of QQ Accounts, 2004–18 84
4.2 Weixin and WeChat Combined Monthly Active Users (MAU) (Millions) 85
4.3 Tencent's Yearly Investments by Region, 2004–18 (RMB Million) 97
4.4 Tencent's Yearly Revenues Outside China, 2009–18 99

Figures

2.1 Tencent's Structure as of June 2004, Before IPO 35
2.2 Tencent's Annual Revenue Growth, 2001–18 37
2.3 Annual Growth in Internet Value-Added Services, 2001–11 (USD in millions) 38
2.4 Annual Growth in Mobile Value-Added Services, 2001–11 (USD in millions) 38
2.5 Annual Growth in Value-Added Services, 2012–18 39
3.1 Tencent's Shareholding Structure Immediately After IPO 68
3.2 Naspers 2018 Revenue by Segment 72
3.3 Naspers 2018 Revenue in Internet Segment 73
3.4 Naspers 2018 Revenue by Region 73
4.1 Tencent's Investments by Regions in 2018 98
4.2 Tencent's Yearly Revenues Outside China, 2009–18 99

Acknowledgments

This book, developed out of my doctoral dissertation, would not have been possible without the mentorship of Dan Schiller. It is such a fortune and luxury to have learned from and worked with Dan. A million times I came out of our conversations feeling energized, enlightened, and recharged. I have also benefited enormously from Robert McChesney's insightful and encouraging guidance. Susan Davis and Yuezhi Zhao are true role models. I admire and will always look up to their upbeat attitudes to scholarship and life.

I am deeply indebted to my dear teachers, colleagues, and friends from the University of Illinois community whose kindness and care carried me through the five-year Ph.D. journey in the Midwestern town of Urbana. I am also lucky to have a political-economy intellectual community across time and space. My special thanks go to Yu Hong, Chunfeng Lin, Xinyu Lu, Bingchun Meng, Hong Shen, and Changchang Wu. Wherever they are their passion, talent, hard work, and friendship would always motivate me to be a fearless critical scholar.

I am grateful for the generous support and nourishment from the School of Interdisciplinary Arts and Sciences at the University of Washington Bothell. I thank Lauren Berliner, Peter Brooks, Bruce Burgett, Ben Gardner, Kristin Gustafson, Susan Harewood, Bill Humphreys, Alka Kurian, Julie Shayne, Mira Shimabukuro, Ana Thompson, Deirdre Vinyard, and Simone Willynck for being great colleagues, mentors, and friends since I joined the IAS family.

I also express my gratitude to Benjamin J. Birkinbine, Rodrigo Gomez, and Janet Wasko, the series editors of Global Media Giants, for inviting me to participate in this project. Erica Wetter and Emma Sherriff, Routledge publishing assistants, have provided great help. I appreciate Mary Lou Kowaleski's consistent copyediting assistance.

I would have not been able to achieve anything without the unconditional love from my parents. I am extremely grateful to my family in China for their care, patience, encouragement, and inspiration. Last but not least, Jianxiong, thank you for being the best companion, comrade, and life partner.

Introduction

The Internet and China have been the two poles of growth in the global political economy for several decades.[1]

The information and communication technology (ICT) industry, which U.S. digital giants dominate, has risen to be one of the most lucrative and powerful industries. The worth of the world's ten largest Internet companies in 2018 was $4.38 trillion, surpassing Germany's 2017 gross domestic product (GDP) and making these companies together the fourth-largest global economy.[2] Apple alone, with a market capitalization of $995.5 billion, stands as number 17 in the World Bank's 2017 GDP ranking—just above Turkey and the Netherlands.[3]

China, on the other hand, has been another dynamic site for capitalist expansion since 1978 when leader Deng Xiaoping opened up China to global capitalism.[4] Two shaping forces were high inbound foreign direct investments (FDI) and trade exports.[5] China's GDP grew by 82 percent from $149.5 billion in 1978 to $12.24 trillion in 2017.[6] China's rise as a global political-economic power should be understood within the more encompassing worldwide process—namely, the neoliberal trend across Global North and South that resulted in structural shifts between the two.[7]

As the global ICT industry and China more and more interact with one another, China's Internet industry comes as a unique site to study the dynamics in contemporary global political economy. This book investigates Tencent, a Chinese Internet company, as a nexus of the two poles of growth: China and the Internet.

The Political Economy of the Internet

Critical political economy, according to Vincent Mosco, is the study of "control and survival in social life." The analytical strength of this approach is to foreground the "social relations, particularly the power relations" at the center of scholarly concerns and to examine the production, distribution, consumption, and regulation of resources—including communication resources—within the circuit of capitalist processes. The political economy of communication, specifically, recognizes the media and communication sector as an integral aspect of the "fundamental economic, political, social and cultural processes" in modern capitalist societies.[8]

Grounded in a historical and critical tradition, political economy of communication (PEC) has contemporary relevance for its critique on the capital-accumulation logic and the commodity fetishism in cultural industry.[9] To answer the question, "Who (controls) and for whom (production, distribution, and audiences)?" borrowing Dallas Smythe's words, PEC cares, first and foremost, about the power relations—both in and outside the media and communication institutions—that have shaped, informed, and challenged their production and distributions.[10] By looking at media and communication institutions as a part of the capitalist system, political economists have inquired into individual media firms as sites where ownership and control, organizational and business strategies, capital structures, product development, research and development (R&D), and public relations (PR) strategies, units of capital, and state entities have interacted.[11]

Carrying forward the basic line of research in power dynamics and social relations, PEC scholars in recent decades have been keenly interested in studying ICTs as spheres of transnational capitalist expansion. As Christian Fuchs states, "The Internet is today primarily a space that is dominated by corporations that derive money profit from human communication."[12]

Herbert Schiller lays out an early foundation of such arguments in his examination of the use of communication technologies and information systems by the United States in maintaining dominant power. He argues that "surveillance, intervention, and marketing are the near-certain outcomes of the utilization of new communication technologies, domestically and globally."[13] Dan Schiller and Robert McChesney consistently work on identifying the extensive commercial power in global information and communication industries under the neoliberal policy framework.[14] Dan Schiller details the historical process and global reconfiguration of the telecommunication sector along neoliberal lines. McChesney examines the mechanisms of advertising, surveillance, and networked corporations that have given rise to "a handful of gigantic monopolistic firms" in the U.S. context.[15] Vincent Mosco looks into one recent development of global information capitalism—cloud computing—which, in his argument, is an "engine that powers informational capitalism" that carries economic, political, social, environmental, and cultural implications.[16] ShinJoung Yeo studies the management and practice of scientific labor in search-engine industry as a critical tool for Google's profitability.[17]

As these scholars' critiques on mainstream Internet studies stand, the Internet is an integral and critical vehicle of the basic power relations and capitalist structure in social processes. Pointed out by McChesney, the foundational mechanisms in contemporary capitalism, such as "profit motive, commercialism, public relations, marketing, and advertising," must be references for comprehending and evaluating how the Internet developed and what forces shaped it.[18]

While these works have set the ground for understanding the political economy of the Internet, they are primarily situated in the United States and the developed world, despite China's increasing importance to the dynamism of the global communication system. Only recently have studies begun about China's Internet companies. The extended case study of Tencent in this book adopts the long-standing political economy approach to the contemporary Chinese context.

Contemporary China and Communication

Many scholars have offered interpretations on China's contemporary transformation. Three major discourses—neoliberalism, developmentalism, and nationalism—are reviewed here.

The first theme pertains to the role of what David Harvey calls neoliberalism in China's reform. Harvey refers to China's transformation "from a closed backwater to an open center of capitalist dynamism," as a "neoliberal project" that readapted to capital accumulation and reenabled the power of economic elites in alliance with political elites.[19] He sees China's experience as part of a global neoliberal wave that has prioritized the practices of liberating corporate freedoms and commercial interests and a withdrawal of the state from many social and public sectors. Critics, however, maintain that such a pure capitalist analysis seems to be inadequate for understanding the practices of China's state. Giovanni Arrighi, for example, finds dual efforts by the Chinese state that, on the one hand, were in favor of capitalist development and, on the other, were concerned with labor welfare.[20]

Instead of the "wholesale neoliberalism" framework, China's path was seen by others as a reflection of internal conflicts and a crisis of Chinese socialism that crystallized on a developmental state model.[21] Alvin Y. So's work finds evidence from China's rebalancing policies that were oriented to social development rather than economic growth.[22] Lin Chun situates the political economy of the Chinese model in the historical and global context of a revolutionary, socialist, and post-socialist path and argues, "Capitalism is neither an inevitable evolutionary stage nor a sustained option for China."[23] Rather, according to Lin, Chinese reform attempts to seek a Chinese alternative to modernity and responses to the crisis of Chinese socialism, although it has to some extent departed from socialism and turned into a capitalist path.

A third perspective, stemming mostly from the Cold War rhetoric, holds a nationalist view that China is a rising national power in global geopolitics that generated not only "fearful reactions" among the Western public but also genuine concerns from Western political leaders.[24] Minqi Li argues that the U.S. hegemony was declining, and China was potentially capable of destabilizing the existing world system.[25] The claim that China was rising as a global power is not unchallenged, though, in that China is only a "partial power" and "has not yet bought the world" according to David Shambaugh and Peter Nolan, respectively.[26]

Among these discussions, the role of China's communication sector in its contemporary development has been a contested one. Traditionally, media and communication in China have been understood, since the revolutionary time, mainly as a means of control. Much analytical emphasis in prior scholarship is put on the state power and the propaganda mechanism.[27] Banal discussions have very often featured a discourse of censorship versus democratization and/or the state-versus-market dichotomies in China's communication practices, assuming that the communist nature of the state would naturally take over the propaganda machine. Such a dichotomous argument holds some element of truth historically but also neglects a changing dialectic of the state and market relations coupling the reform.[28]

In recent years, an increasing number of researchers have started recognizing communication and, especially, the ICT industries in China as critical aspects in the country's political-economic (re)structuring. Yuezhi Zhao, as the groundbreaking scholar, argues that the political economy of China's communication is one essential perspective of understanding the "class character of the Chinese state and its role in the shifting regimes of capitalist accumulation."[29] In her earlier work, Zhao demonstrates the nuanced nature of the relation between Chinese news media and the communist party–state apparatus and unveils the multidimensional dynamics of the state and capital interaction, foregrounding their entangled relations in communications, and pointing to the inadequacy of the equations between commercialization and democratization and the dichotomous discourse of "state or market." According to Zhao, the state and capital, in collaboration and contestation, have shaped "the institutions, processes and contents of contemporary Chinese communication."[30]

With respect to the newly developed ICT and Internet sector, in particular, PEC scholars further situate it in China's contemporary reinsertion into global capitalism.[31] Yu Hong extends the inquiry into the political economy of ICTs by exploring state-business relations in designing and constructing China's information infrastructure systems.[32] Hong argues that the information communication sector is interwoven into the state's information policies that prioritized continuing capitalist (re)production. Emerging scholars add knowledge to latest developments in Internet industry from different perspectives, such as policy shifts and financial connections.[33]

China's communication sector, particularly the ICT industries, is the critical lenses through which we are able to understand how contemporary China's development continues to pivot.[34]

Methods and Organization of the Study

This book is built on a political economy case study of a leading Chinese Internet company, Tencent. Taking Tencent as a historically unfolding business entity, the book focuses on the shaping, enabling, and conditioning forces with which the company has developed, rather than considering individual user behaviors, employee performances, or isolated management strategies. Referring to the strengths of PEC scholarship, the book proposes four lines of inquiry:

- The regulatory context within which Tencent developed
- Tencent's economic profile, such as corporate structure, financial performance, scopes of businesses, and expansion strategies
- Tencent's political profile, including the founders' backgrounds, the company's ownership and control, and directorship connections
- Tencent's cultural profile, highlighting popular products, such as QQ, WeChat, and gaming development

The study draws upon document research, using primary and secondary sources that include the following four types:

- Policy documents from Chinese government entities: the State Council, Ministry of Industry and Information Technology (MIIT), China Internet Network Information Center, and National Development and Reform Commission, and others
- Corporate annual reports, quarterly reports, and other forms of trade releases from Tencent and other related companies, as stock exchange markets request from their listed companies
- News reports and analysis of Internet and ICT industries from financial and business sources and trade journals
- Reports that professional investment analysts from banks and/or consultancy firms issue

These four types of sources go far to contextualize and clarify the research questions. But they embody various weaknesses, since they are expressions of special interests and power relations, and therefore require caution in use and analysis.

The rest of the book is organized as follows: Chapter 1 goes into the historical context of the birth and growth of China's Internet and Tencent.

Chapter 2 describes Tencent's economic features: capital structure, basic businesses and expansion strategy, horizontal and vertical integration, and diversification. Chapter 3 delves into the company's ownership, control, and its primary institutional stakeholder, the South Africa-based media conglomerate Naspers. Chapter 4 directs attention to the cultural sphere by examining mobile chat and digital gaming, two of Tencent's most popular and successful products and services. The conclusion summarizes Tencent's rise as a global digital giant grown out of the joint efforts by the Chinese state and transnational financial capital. This book contributes to the political-economy theory of the Internet, to the knowledge of China's contemporary transformation and ICT industry, and to the understanding of two emerging and entangling trends in global political economy: transnationalization and financialization.

Notes

1. Dan Schiller, "Poles of Market Growth? Open Questions About China, Information, and the World Economy," *Global Media and Communication* 1, no. 1 (2005): 79–103.
2. Shobhit Seth, "World's Top 10 Internet Companies," *Investopedia*, October 2018, accessed January 8, 2019, www.investopedia.com/articles/personal-finance/030415/worlds-top-10-internet-companies.asp; Prableen Bajpai, "The World's Top 20 Economies," *Investopedia*, January 2, 2019, accessed January 8, 2019, www.investopedia.com/insights/worlds-top-economies/.
3. World Bank, "GDP Ranking," n.d., accessed January 8, 2019, https://datacatalog.worldbank.org/dataset/gdp-ranking.
4. Peter Nolan, *Is China Buying the World* (Malden, MA: Polity, 2012); Yuezhi Zhao and Dan Schiller, "Dances with Wolves? China's Integration into Digital Capitalism," *Info* 3, no. 2 (2001): 137–51; David Harvey, *A Brief History of Neoliberalism* (Oxford: Oxford University Press, 2005); Dan Schiller, *Digital Depression: Information Technology and Economic Crisis* (Urbana-Champaign: University of Illinois Press, 2014).
5. Harvey, *Brief History*, 134–42.
6. "40 Years After Reform and Opening-Up: China's GDP 1978–2017," *Global Times*, May 23, 2018, accessed January 9, 2018, www.globaltimes.cn/content/1103708.shtml.
7. Jan Nederveen Pieterse, "Representing the Rise of the Rest as Threat," *Global Media & Communication* 5, no. 2 (2009): 221–37.
8. Vincent Mosco, *The Political Economy of Communication: Rethinking and Renewal* (London: Sage, 2009), 2–3, 24, 66.
9. Robert McChesney, *Communication Revolution: Critical Junctures and the Future of Media* (New York: New Press, 2007), 53–55.
10. Dallas Walker Smythe, "On the Political Economy of Communications," *Journalism & Mass Communication Quarterly* 37 (1960): 563–72.
11. Noobar R. Danielian, *AT&T: The Story of Industrial Conquest* (New York: Vanguard, 1939); Graham Murdock and Peter Golding, "For a Political Economy of Mass Communications," *Socialist Register* 10 (1973): 205–34; Janet Wasko, *Hollywood in the Information Age: Beyond the Silver Screen* (Austin: University

of Texas Press, 1995); Edward S. Herman and Robert W. McChesney, *The Global Media: The New Missionaries of Corporate Capitalism* (London: Cassell, 1997); Janet Wasko, *Understanding Disney: The Manufacture of Fantasy* (Cambridge: Polity, 2001).

12. Christian Fuchs, *Foundations of Critical Media and Information Studies* (London: Routledge, 2011), 337.
13. Herbert Schiller, *Information and the Crisis Economy* (Norwood, NJ: Ablex, 1984), 23.
14. Dan Schiller, *Digital Capitalism: Networking the Global Market System* (Cambridge, MA: MIT Press, 1999).
15. Robert McChesney, *Digital Disconnect: How Capitalism Is Turning the Internet Against Democracy* (New York: New Press, 2013), 20.
16. Vincent Mosco, *To the Cloud: Big Data in a Turbulent World* (Boulder, CO: Paradigm, 2014).
17. ShinJoung Yeo, "Behind the Search Box: The Political Economy of a Global Internet Industry" (Unpublished PhD diss., University of Illinois, Urbana-Champaign, 2014).
18. McChesney, *Digital Disconnect*, 20.
19. Harvey, *Brief History*, 122.
20. Giovanni Arrighi, *Adam Smith in Beijing: Lineages of the Twenty-First Century* (London: Verso, 2007), 24.
21. Yongnian Zheng, *Globalization and State Transformation in China* (Cambridge: Cambridge University Press, 2004), 174.
22. Alvin Y. So, "Rethinking the Chinese Developmental Miracle," in *China and the Transformation of Global Capitalism*, ed. Ho-fung Huang (Baltimore: John Hopkins University Press, 2009), 50–64.
23. Lin Chun, *China and Global Capitalism: Reflections on Marxism, History, and Contemporary Politics* (New York: Palgrave Pivot, 2013), 198.
24. Elena Barabantseva, "In Pursuit of an Alternative Model? The Modernisation Trap in China's Official Development Discourse," *East Asia* 29, no. 1 (2012): 63–79; Nolan, *Is China Buying the World*, 2–3.
25. Minqi Li, *The Rise of China and the Demise of the Capitalist World-Economy* (New York: Monthly Review, 2008), 176–77.
26. David Shambaugh, *China Goes Global: The Partial Power* (Oxford: Oxford University Press, 2013), 6; Nolan, Is *China Buying the World*, 66, 143.
27. Qiuqing Tai, "China's Media Censorship: A Dynamic and Diversified Regime," *Journal of East Asian Studies* 14 (2014): 185–209.
28. Chin-Chuan Lee, Zhou He, and Yu Huang, "Chinese Party Publicity Inc. Conglomerated: The Case of the Shenzhen Press Group," *Media, Culture, & Society* 28, no. 4 (2006); Susan Shirk, *Changing Media, Changing China* (New York: Oxford University Press, 2011), 1–2.
29. Yuezhi Zhao, "The Challenge of China: Contribution to a Transcultural Political Economy of Communication for the Twenty-First Century," in *The Handbook of Political Economy of Communication*, eds. Janet Wasko, Graham Murdock, and Helena Sousa (Chichester: Wiley-Blackwell, 2011), 564.
30. Ibid., 11.
31. Yu Hong, *Labor, Class Formation, and China's Informationized Policy of Economic Development* (Lanham, MD: Lexington, 2011); Yu Hong, "Reading the Twelfth Five-Year Plan: China's Communication-Driven Mode of Economic Restructuring," *International Journal of Communication* 5 (2011): 1045–57; D. Schiller, "Poles of Market Growth"; D. Schiller, *Digital Depression*.

32. Yu Hong, *Networking China* (Urbana-Champaign: University of Illinois Press, 2017).
33. Hong Shen, "Across the Great (Fire) Wall: China and the Global Internet" (Unpublished doctoral diss., University of Illinois, Urbana-Champaign, 2017); Jing Wang, "Stir-Frying Internet Finance: Financialization and the Institutional Role of Financial News in China," *International Journal of Communication* 11 (2017): 581–602; Lianrui Jia and Dwayne Winseck, "The Political Economy of Chinese Internet Companies: Financialization, Concentration, and Capitalization," *International Communication Gazette* 80, no. 1 (2018): 30–59.
34. D. Schiller, *Digital Depression*, 229–31.

1 History and Context

In May 1994 the first full Internet operation under TCP/IP protocol in China was established through a direct connection to the American telecommunication company Sprint.[1] Also that year, the first web server and the first set of web pages in China were launched at the Institute of High Energy Physics, one of the research institutions under the Chinese Academy of Sciences.[2] The number of Internet users in China grew from 620,000 in 1997 to 8.9 million in 2000.[3]

Fast-forward to 2018. On November 11, 2018, Alibaba, China's largest e-commerce company, kicked off Singles Day shopping festival, a Chinese version of the American black Friday, with a four-hour gala. "Double 11"—a play on how the number 1 represents being single and unmarried—was reinvented by Alibaba as a shopping event for young consumers. The event in past years has featured many international stars, such as Kevin Spacey, Adam Lambert, Daniel Craig, Miranda Kerr, and numerous Chinese celebrities. Throughout the performances, promotional activities—drawings for free items and gift money, and discounts on various products—were used to stimulate the audience's purchasing desire. The gross merchandise value of the 2018 shopping day hit a record high of $30.8 billion in sales.[4]

In a little over two decades, the Internet in China has become a gigantic platform for communication, mobilization, and commercialization. Tracing China's Internet from its birth through its major stages of growth will help to understand how.

A brief conceptual discussion will be useful. Several scholars have written about the history of China's ICTs and Internet. Milton Muller, Tan Zixiang, and Wu Wei have discussed the early development of the telecom and data network, with the network building efforts primarily from the Chinese government. Some other scholars have interests in the issue of censorship and control. It is no new argument that China's Internet was censored by the state and self-censored by the service and content providers.[5] Alongside this discussion is a concern for the democratic potential the Internet might bring to China.[6] One explanation for the scholarly attention to China's Internet is that this interest is motivated by the prospect that the Internet could be a democratizing force in a communist regime famously known for censoring media and public opinion.[7] The seemingly opposite themes of censorship and democracy actually represent two ends of one central assumption that the Internet is just a tool for enlightenment or suppression. Granting that such argument has some validity, it at its best provides an inaccurate and incomplete account of the digital landscape in China and at its worst invites an oversimplification of the complex social interaction and a neglect of the subjectivities of different agencies and institutions in China. The Internet itself does not stand as an "anonymous, decentralized, borderless and interactive" system for "diverse opinions, civic activities or collective actions."[8] It is the power relation and social dynamic in a system—be it a capitalist or socialist or a mix—that is decisive for the structure of information and communication technology (ICT).

ICT and Internet sectors are not only communication tools or platforms but also integral aspects of the capitalist system. The ICT industry in China has been oriented, in several ways, toward capitalist development, which this chapter examines. It focuses on the historical and regulatory contexts as they not only informed and institutionalized the system of information provision but also reflected the existing power negotiations that have devised the policies. Communication policies respond, to different extents, to some profound questions concerning "the nature of the media system and how it is structured, and how that might affect the conditions for the informational needs of a democracy."[9] More critically, the agendas set by policies are "expressions of dynamic processes and power relations" in a society.[10] In China the party-state is one of the most important, though not the only important, powers in setting forward how the emerging communication system is structured.[11] Through the prism of policy discourse, we can better understand the political-economic rationales and how relations between different institutions played out in China's Internet development, laying foundations for private companies like Tencent.

This chapter first traces the history of the building of network infrastructure and services in China, with special attention paid to questions of when and to what extent domestic private capital was allowed into the Internet industry. The Internet in China developed in four distinct stages, and not long after its birth, China's Internet was embedded in the country's capitalist development and global reinsertion through industrialization and informatization. Both as an enabling condition and an outcome, priority was given to building the information network and industry in coastal and urban areas, which contributed to not only the creation of an enormous pool of migrant labor but also to the user base for new Internet services and applications. Throughout, the chapter shows that China's ICT industry and capitalist investments mutually constituted and facilitated each other's development under the evolving central government policies, and together industry, investment, and government gave birth to Tencent.

Building a Chinese Internet

The Chinese central government's policies on Internet development and the efforts in building the information superhighway went through four stages: the preparation, 1987 to 1993; the Internet as infrastructure, 1994 and 1995; the Internet as industrialization, 1996 to 2010; and the Internet as a pillar industry, 2011 to the present. Throughout these processes, capital has been visible, but different units of capital—state-owned units and private ones—were allowed to enter the industry to different extents. In the two early stages, the driving force came primarily from state-owned capital backed by the central government's informatization policies. Private capital and foreign capital were given more space in the latest two stages, which reflected China's further opening up and integrating into global capitalism. These stages were also parallel to China's overall political-economic transformation since the 1980s. In 1978 not only had the central government in China decided to liberalize and open up the domestic economy but it also rediscovered the foundational position of science and technology in boosting economic productivity.[12] The Internet's second stage of development came along with China's then top leader Deng Xiaoping's southern tour to Shenzhen among other southern coastal cities in 1992, during which he affirmed the opening-up policies to further connect with the worldwide market economy and to use foreign capital to facilitate domestic growth.[13] The third stage broadly correlated with an era when China sought to aggressively reintegrate into global capitalism by using ICTs both as a channel for communication and a vehicle for attracting investments, while more recent developments came under the country's post-crisis rebalancing.

Preparation: 1987–1993

The first stage was the preparation years between 1987 and 1993, during which policies were focused on encouraging scientific research and popularizing networking technology.[14] This period was marked by two milestones, with primary efforts from the Chinese government-funded science-and-technology research institutes and universities. The first event, in September 1987, was the first e-mail message—"Across the great wall, we can reach every corner in the world"—sent across China's borders.[15] This message, sent when China was still considered by many as a closed, authoritarian land, signaled that researchers could exchange e-mail communication with foreign educational institutions.[16] A second turning point was in 1994 when the first full Internet operation under TCP/IP protocol in China was, for the first time, up and running.[17] This meant that China started enjoying "full general Internet connectivity beyond just e-mail" by making a direct connection between China and the United States.[18]

In this period, the Chinese government gave priority to network development in preparation for the launch and upgrade of national information infrastructure, the work of which was mostly based in research and educational institutions. For example, the academy network of Chinese Academy of Sciences (CASNET) and the campus networks of Tsinghua University (TUNET) and Peking University (PUNET) were all constructed during this time.[19] Not much emphasis was put on the economic potential of the Internet during this stage.

The Internet as Infrastructure: 1994 and 1995

The second stage, during 1994 and 1995, saw a wave of construction of the basic network infrastructures by academic institutions, government agencies, and, occasionally, some primary commercial carriers.[20] The Internet was primarily seen as a platform and tool for communicating and disseminating information to facilitate industrialization in major agrarian and industrial sectors. By the end of 1995, China had "10 national networks, 41 leading governmental information services in electronic form, 16 news sources in electronic form, 43 university-based World Wide Web servers and information producers, and 52 commercial information products prepared by electronic information producers."[21]

One example of such effort was the China Education and Research Network (CERNET), a nationwide backbone network to connect the campus networks of universities and research institutions.[22] The State Development Planning Commission, China's National Science Foundation, and China's State Education Commission initiated and funded the project, which was officially approved in August 1994.[23] CERNET's demonstration project, completed by the end of 1995, made it the leading network in China in terms of backbone speed and range of coverage, reaching more than a hundred universities in China and covering all mainland provinces except Tibet.[24] CERNET also provided an international connection to global academic networks through a 128K international special line to the U.S. Internet.[25]

Another nationwide backbone network was ChinaNET, led by the Ministry of Posts and Telecommunications (MPT) and carried out by its Directorate General of Telecommunications, an office in charge of providing national telecommunications services.[26] ChinaNET offered international links in three major cities—Beijing, Shanghai, and Guangzhou—by working with Sprint.[27] Spearheading China's information-highway project and prioritizing service provision to the three largest cities at the time, MPT became the leader in providing commercial Internet services.[28] By 1995 ChinaNET was the largest commercial Internet service provider in China.[29]

Although the commercial value of the Internet was starting to get some attention, the priority of central government in this period was to facilitate public information exchange and support macro level economic planning and administration via an effective and reliable information infrastructure.[30] In March 1993 vice premier Zhu Rongji initiated the Golden Bridge Project, a national network for public economic information; in August the State Council of the People's Republic of China approved a $3 million budget to build it; and in June 1994 the State Council issued a notice to expand the Golden Bridge Project into three golden projects.[31] The additional two projects were the Golden Gateway, a central information system of foreign trade and import-export management, and the Golden Card, a central financing, banking, and credit card system.[32] As these three projects were effective in providing key information and assisting the central government's economic planning, coordinating, and managing, in 1995 more golden projects for various industries were brought into being—Golden Tax, Golden Enterprise, and Golden Agriculture, among others.[33] Serving primarily as communication channels of information for policymaking in different industries, these networks strengthened the central government's coordinating power.[34]

The Internet as Industrialization: 1996–2010

The 15 years between 1996 and 2010 constituted a third stage during which the Internet and information industries were intensively developed as vehicles for economic growth. In the prior stage, information technology was used in selected primary and secondary industries for their growth. In this third stage, instead of being merely a tool, ICTs became important in their own right for the country's industrialization. This stage pivoted on a set of distinctive changes in industrial structure and government structure.

First, on the industrial landscape, in January 1996, during its 42nd meeting, the State Council approved a provisional directive on the management of international Internet connections in China, which endorsed the MPT as the official leader in the country's Internet business: "All international computer networking traffic, both incoming and outgoing, must go through telecommunication channels provided by the Ministry of Posts and Telecommunications."[35] MPT's Directorate General of Telecommunications was renamed China Telecom and restructured as a state-owned enterprise under China's 1995 telecom reform. This was the first time the Chinese government regulated the use of the Internet, an indication of its growing importance.[36] According to the directive, the government was in charge of the planning work and protocols for all international computer connections.

All existing networks were subject to MPT supervision and that of the Ministry of Electronics Industry (MEI), the State Education Commission, and the Chinese Academy of Sciences for the management of general Internet traffic, computer companies, and education and research institutions, respectively.[37] The country was making necessary preparations for advancing technology in the national economy. The regulation also highlighted that all the international information traffic—both incoming and outgoing—had to go through MPT's telecom network and under the government's scrutiny.[38] This showed that the Chinese state was open in embracing foreign flows of information and, simultaneously, cautious in encountering potentially different and antagonistic thoughts and ideologies, as this was at a time when the overall national economy was transforming into an outward- and export-oriented mode, and the international flows of information and capital were becoming both necessary and preferable.[39]

Following this provision, in March 1996 the National People's Congress approved the Outline of the Ninth Five-Year Plan (1996–2000) for National Economic and Social Development and Long-Range Objectives to the Year 2010 (hereafter referred to as the Outline), in which the phrase "information technology and informatization for economic development" for the first time appeared, and the growth of computer and Internet technology was an integral goal for the next five years' economic and social development.[40] The Five-Year Plans, to be sure, were a series of social and economic development initiatives designed by the central Chinese government, the first of which began in 1953. It was in this very Outline that the government proposed that a socialist market economy was to take shape initially in the five-year frame of 1996 to 2000: "Positive but cautious steps must be taken to foster a comparatively perfect money market as well as markets in such key areas as real estate, labor, technology and information."[41] Specifically, technology and information were utilized to achieve readjustment of the industrial structure from an extensive mode—one that emphasized "aggrandizement of the total size"—to an intensive one that highlighted "the efficiency in utilizing each unit of input in production or allocation."[42] Furthermore, the Outline discussed the role of various economic elements and capital units from different sectors, as well as the investment system and fund-raising scheme in the market.[43] In particular, it articulated that the nonpublic elements, that is, individuals and private actors, should be strengthened to supplement the public ownership-dominated economy system.[44] This meant that further reform was to take place, where private units were allowed gradually to participate in the national economy. It was under such context that China's Internet industry blossomed. In other words, the development of information technology and Internet came under the central government's umbrella agenda of deepening the country's market economy reform and opening-up process.[45]

Echoing the Outline, the State Council's Information Work Leading Group held its first national meeting on the issue of informatization in 1997 and announced the Ninth Five-Year Plan for Informatization and Long-Range Objectives to the Year 2010. The Plan specifically called for "joint efforts" by the state and other economic elements to build the Internet and information sectors.[46]

The five-year period of the Ninth Five-Year Plan saw a great amount of government funding in information infrastructure and technological innovation. A $12.24 billion (RMB 101.5 billion) investment was put into building special zones for high-tech development, where 17,000 high-tech enterprises were in operation and more than 2.2 million people were employed between 1996 and 2000. Another $385 million (RMB 3.19 billion) was used for "technical innovation projects in the industrial sector."[47] As a result, the national economy output and especially that of information industries witnessed huge surges. The gross output value of electronic information products manufacture (software manufacture included) increased from $29.43 billion (RMB 245.7 billion) in 1995 to $93.87 billion (RMB 778.2 billion) in 1999, while the gross value of general communication services grew from $11.84 billion (RMB 98.9 billion) in 1995 to $25.49 billion (RMB 211.3 billion) in 1999.[48] According to a *China Daily* report, those 17,000 high-tech enterprises in special high-tech development zones contributed an industrial added value of $17.8 billion (RMB 147.6 billion) and an export trading volume of $12 billion.[49]

A second change in this period was the administrative reform and restructuring of central government agencies that regulated the management and businesses of the Internet. As early as December 1993, the central government named an interdepartmental task force for joint leadership on issues of "informatization for economic development," chaired by then vice premier Zou Jiahua.[50] This task force of the State Economic Informatization Joint Meeting was renamed the Information Work Leading Group and under the State Council. With Zou still acting as the head of the office, the Information Work Leading Group was coordinated by staff members from 19 ministerial departments, commissions, and bureaus.[51] In 1999 the State Council set up a National Information Work Leading Group, chaired by then vice premier Wu Bangguo with staff members from 13 ministerial departments, commissions, and bureaus.[52] The added term "national" suggests the importance the central government attached to information for industrialization. Premiers Zhu Rongji and Wen Jiabao subsequently took charge of this leading group. The National Information Work Leading Group was closed in 2008, when the "superministry reform" took place, and was merged into the newly established Ministry of Industry and Information Technology (MIIT) as part of its information technology promotion division. In 2014, however, the central government, under the leadership of president Xi Jinping, founded a new office—the Central Leading Group for Cyberspace Affairs and the Cyberspace Administration of China—to enhance China's Internet security and strengthen the informatization strategy.[53] The Central Leading Group for Cyberspace Affairs has carried forward the heritage from State Council's previous joint task forces and also aimed to respond to the opportunities and challenges in the new era, since paramount importance was put on Internet and ICTs as the new pillar industry for national economy.[54]

Another aspect of this governmental restructuring involved changes to ministries that regulated the Internet and information industry. Historically, MPT operated and managed the information and communication services.[55] Although central government agencies had always fought for control over this lucrative sector, the rivalry became especially intense when the MEI set foot in telecommunication services by launching China United Telecommunications Corp. (China Unicom) in 1993 jointly with two other ministries—Ministry of Railway and Ministry of Electronic Power.[56] MEI later formed another telecom company, Ji Tong, which built on the ministry's strength in equipment manufacturing.[57] In view of an increasing overlap and interconnection between electronics and the information industries, the central government reorganized MPT and MEI and formed one ministry, the Ministry of Information Industry (MII) in 1998.[58] This reorganization, aiming at facilitating economic transitions and enhancing administrative efficiency, spoke to the centerpiece of the state's policies at this time—the Internet and information for industrialization.[59] In 2008 the ministerial reform continued, and the newly formed MIIT incorporated the functions of several central agencies: MII; National Development and Reform Commission (NDRC); the Commission of Science, Technology, and Industry for National Defense, except their oversight of nuclear power management; and the State Council's Informatization Office.[60] In addition to the changes in the ministry titles, the reconstitution of the MIIT as a more comprehensive entity reflected a further integration of informatization and industrialization.[61]

As a result of these changes in the industrial and governmental dimensions and the progress made during the Ninth Five-Year Plan period, the Tenth and Eleventh Five-Year Plans kept readjusting industrial structure and assigning more weight to the Internet and ICTs. Growth was little short of explosive. By the end of 2005, the total gross income of the information industry reached $537 billion (RMB 4.4 trillion)—4.6 times the figure in 2000—and the industry's added value in national GDP increased from 4 percent in 2000 to 7.2 percent.[62] Between 2006 and 2010, a total of $188 billion (RMB 1.5 trillion) was put in the telecommunication industry, with 40 percent of investment for broadband construction.[63] By the end of 2010, the sales of the information industry topped $1.15 trillion (RMB 7.8 trillion).[64] ICT and Internet businesses expanded as a driving force for innovation and development in other industries, as well as a core industry themselves.[65]

Table 1.1 Annual Gross Income in Chinese Telecom Industry

Year	*Billion RMB*	*Billion USD*
2000	341	41.2
2001	415	50.1
2002	463	56
2003	517	62.5
2004	573	69.3
2005	637	77.8
2006	712	89
2007	805	105.9
2008	814	118
2009	871	128
2010	899	132.8
2011	1,066	165
2012	1,186	188
2013	1,169	188.9
2014	1,154	187.9
2015	1,125	181.5
2016	1,189	180.2
2017	1,262	185.6
2018	1,301	194.36

Source: MIIT Annual Statistics on Telecommunications (www.miit.gov.cn/n1146312/n1146904/n1648372/index.html).

Table 1.2 Annual Sales Income in Chinese Electronic Information Industry

Year	*Electronics Manufacturing*		*Software Service*		*Total*	
	Billion RMB	*Billion USD*	*Billion RMB*	*Billion USD*	*Billion RMB*	*Billion USD*
2001	1,136.4	137.4	51.6	6.2	1,188	143.7
2002	1,334	161.3	66	8	1,400	169.3
2003	NA					
2004	2,801	338.7	278	33.6	3,079	372.3
2005	3,451	421.4	390	47.6	3,841	469
2006	4,270	535.8	480	60.2	4,750	596
2007	4,543	597.8	583	76.7	5,126	674.5
2008	5,125	738.5	757	109.1	5,882	847.6
2009	5,131	751.2	951	139.2	6,082	890.5
2010	6,340	936.5	1,300	192	7,800[1]	1,152
2011	7,491	1,160	1,847	286	9,338	1,446
2012	8,462	1,341	2,479	393	10,941	1,734
2013	9,320	1,505	31,000	500	12,400	2,003
2014	10,299	1,677	3,700	603	14,000	2,280
2015	11,132	1,787	4,285	688	15,400	2,473
2016	12,189	1,836	4,823	726	17,000	2,562
2017	13,000	1,926	5,510	816	18,510	2,742
2018	14,170	2,140	6,306	953	20,476	3,093

Sources: MIIT Statistics on Electronic Information Industry and Software Industry (www.miit.gov.cn/n1146312/n1146904/n1648373/index.html; www.miit.gov.cn/n1146312/n1146904/n1648374/index.html).

1 Hereafter, some of the numbers were round up in the original statistical reports.

The Internet as a Pillar Industry: 2011–present

A fourth turning point took place in the wake of 2007–8 financial crisis, when the Internet industry was given added weight by the state. This is a still-ongoing process in which the Internet industry itself has become the backbone of the economy.

Since China's 1978 opening-up and market reforms, the country's spectacular economic growth largely has depended on foreign direct investment and trade export.[66] The achievements are stunning. By 2010, China was the world's largest exporter of goods, contributing to 26.53 percent of the country's GDP and accounting for 9.6 percent of all global exports and, especially, the world's largest exporter of consumer electronic products.[67] However, as many have noted, "in the complex global supply lines of multinational corporations, China primarily occupies the role of final assembler of manufactured goods to be sold in the rich economies."[68] Despite its leadership in bulk, there was an Achilles's heel in such an outward-oriented economic mode—high dependence on the global supply chain. Famously known as a "world factory," China did not possess the core competitiveness for a domestically strong and innovative ICT industry.[69] Moreover, the fast growth rate in GDP from this foreign investment-driven and export-oriented growth model was accompanied by a series of social problems crystallizing on social inequalities, regional imbalances, massive unemployment, and environmental problems.[70] All these problems, aggravated by the 2007–8 global financial crisis, acted as a wake-up call to the Chinese state that its economic advancement held multifaceted consequences and needed to be revised.

In this context, at the 2011 National People's Congress meeting, the central government designated the Internet and ICT sector as *the* pillar industry in national economic restructuring.[71] The Twelfth Five-Year Plan, approved in that meeting, highlighted that to boost domestic consumption by capitalizing on the Internet was a priority. One of the core messages in the Twelfth Five-Year Plan was to cultivate and promote strategic industries of ICTs for a "modern production structure."[72] This signaled a further integration of private businesses with ICTs and an ever-interweaving relation between the state and different units of capital. During the Twelfth Five-Year Plan period, from 2011 to 2015, improved Internet infrastructures and widening diffusion of the mobile Internet brought forward a prosperous Internet economy. In 2014 Internet businesses alone accounted for 7 percent of national GDP, while the market value of Internet companies amounted to $1.24 trillion (RMB 7.85 trillion) and occupied 25.6 percent of China's stock market.[73] As of 2015, 328 China-based Internet companies were publicly listed, with 61 in the United States, 55 in Hong Kong, and 209 in China in Shanghai and Shenzhen.[74] E-commerce, in particular, became a new driving force for trade and consumption. In 2017 the income of e-commerce platforms was $32.23 billion (RMB 218.8 billion) with "a year-on-year increase of 43.4%," and online retail transactions were worth $1.06 trillion (RMB 7.18 trillion).[75]

In the midst of restructuring, the latest policy discourse of Internet Plus further upgraded this pillar industry. The term Internet Plus refers to the state's plan to build a network of banks, financial services, e-commerce, entertainment, and other daily services around the Internet-based technologies, including using mobile Internet, cloud computing, and big-data techniques.[76]

The concept was first reported in premier Li Keqiang's 2015 Report on the Work of the Government. Reflecting the desire for a dynamic and expansive Internet industry, the policy was matched by top leaders' high-profile visits to the Internet companies, "Taobao villages," and high-tech start-up firms created since Xi Jinping's and Li's Keqiang's inaugurations. With an overarching agenda to restructure the general national political economy around the Internet, the purpose of Chinese central government also went beyond economic.[77] In July 2015 the State Council issued Instruction on Actively Promoting Internet Plus Strategy, which promotes using Internet as a stage to advance public services, with a goal to integrate every aspect of society into a networked China by 2018.[78]

To recap, China's Internet experienced four stages of development: the years between 1987 and 1993 were the preparation stage, when multiple research teams under government funding were exploring ways of building a domestic network and connecting to the world. During 1994 and 1995 massive network infrastructure construction was underway as the Internet was primarily seen as a platform where information can be collected and distributed to facilitate central planning and agrarian and industrial development. From 1996 to 2010, as China was reinserting itself into transnational capitalism, the domestic Internet industry evolved as an important vector that generated extraordinary GDP growth. The latest stage elevated the Internet to the pillar industry as the core of the national political economy in the wake of the 2007–8 global financial crisis. Overall, grasping the worldwide moment of the "modernization and globalization of communication networks and the rapid diffusion of powerful information technology," the Chinese government designed policies that gradually integrated the Internet into the national political economy.[79]

Prioritizing Capitalist Pursuit and Urban Development

To facilitate the changing industrial structure, an important shift in policies regarding private capital has taken place since the 1990s.[80] That was to unleash nonstate elements into building information and Internet infrastructures. With the opening of domestic stock markets in Shanghai and Shenzhen in 1991 and 1992, private and, particularly, financial capital became major players in China's economy. As a crucial reminder, there have been some ambiguities and contentions in the definition of private ownership. While the Chinese government defined a private company as "a for-profit organization owned by one or more individuals and employing more than eight people," as Edward Tse points out, this definition excludes a number of business governance structures (such as companies with less than eight employees) or collectively owned businesses (such as Haier and Huawei) or foreign private capital-invested enterprises (such as Alibaba and Tencent).[81] For simplicity and clarity, in the following analysis, private capital is referred to generally as non-state-owned companies that Chinese individuals initially formed and operated. The statistics that follow also refer to private enterprises as "enterprises established by a natural person or majority owned by a natural person" in China.[82]

Despite that the blurry definition and variations in practices made a precise measurement of its size difficult, some general numbers reveal the advance of China's private capital.[83] According to China's National Bureau of Statistics, in 1996 there were 443,000 registered private companies, which accounted for less than 20 percent of all enterprises; in 2012 the number of private companies reached 5.918 million, which accounted for more than 70 percent of all firms.[84] The private companies' shares in China's export increased from almost 0 in 1996 to 39 percent in 2013.[85] Under the central government's guidance to allow various business elements into the national economy, private capital has flourished and changed the industrial dynamics.[86]

Particularly in the Internet industry, value-added service (VAS) providers and content providers started to emerge. Almost no official record exists on the exact number, size, and scale of private companies established at that time. While it is difficult to present a comprehensive evaluation, some anecdotal writings allow a glimpse of the "Internet gold rush." In 1995 Chinapage—an online yellow-page listing of Chinese businesses and products and founded by Jack Ma, AsiaInfo's ChinaNet, Zhong Wang, and Ying HaiWei—came into being.[87] Between 1996 and 2000, many companies that became better-known in the future were founded. In 1996 Charles Zhang established Sohu.com; in 1997 William Lei Ding launched NetEase, offering one of China's earliest free e-mail services; 1998 and 1999 subsequently saw the births of Sina, Tencent, Sohu, NetEase, Jingdong, Ctrip, Baidu, and Alibaba—to name a few.[88] Some of these became extraordinarily successful, and issuing an initial public offering (IPO) on overseas stock exchange markets became a popular option for them. The processes generated complex and often profitable financial structures. As of 2018, seven of them—Tencent, Sohu, NetEase, Jingdong, Ctrip, Baidu, and Alibaba—remain among China's top ten Internet companies.[89] The emergence of

Table 1.3 Chinese Internet Companies Founded Between 1995 and 2000

Company	*Year Founded*	*Year of IPO*	*Listing*	*Business*
Sohu	1996	2000	NASDAQ	Online portal
NetEase	1997	2000	NASDAQ	Online community
Sina	1998	2000	NASDAQ	Online media
ChinaCache	1998	2010	NASDAQ	Content delivery
JD.com (Jingdong)	1998	2014	NASDAQ	E-commerce
Tencent	1998	2004	HKEX	Value-added service
Ctrip	1999	2003	NASDAQ	Online travel agency
Fang.com	1999	2010	NYSE	Online real-estate
Alibaba	1999	2014	NYSE	E-commerce
Baidu	2000	2005	NASDAQ	Search
Bitauto	2000	2010	NYSE	Online automobile

Sources: NASDAQ and NYSE company lists.

these Chinese Internet companies was almost at the same time as the Internet boom in the United States.

With the massive flow of foreign and domestic investments, at the same time, there came the changing landscapes of urban/rural dynamics and population structures, as both a precursor and result of the political-economic shifts that gave rise to China's Internet industry. Specifically, two major shifts took place: the formation of special economic zones (SEZ) and the growing urban, middle, and working classes, who composed a majority of the workforce for and users of ICTs.

Special Economic Zones

During the early years of China's reform, the Chinese government designated two coastal provinces—Guangdong and Fujian—to be the frontrunners in attracting foreign investment, developing industrial clusters, and enjoying favorable policies.[90] In 1980 four cities in these two provinces—Shenzhen, Zhuhai, Shantou, and Xiamen—were designated as special economic zones (SEZs).[91] According to the Regulation on Special Economic Zones in Guangdong Province,

> The enterprise income tax rate in the special zones is 15 percent. Special preferential treatment shall be given to enterprises established within two years of the promulgation of these Regulations, enterprises with an investment US$5 million or more, and enterprises involving higher technology or having a longer period of capital turnover.[92]

Immediate economic effects were documented in just the first few years of the openings of SEZs. In 1981 the four SEZs attracted 59.8 percent of inward foreign direct investment (FDI) to China, with Shenzhen alone accounting for 50.6 percent.[93] In 1984 after China started opening more coastal regions for special economic treatment, these four SEZs still accounted for 26 percent of the nation's FDI, totaling $707.58 million.[94] Witnessing the momentous growth of SEZs, the central government started establishing economic and technological development zones (ETDZs). Between 1984 and 1988, 14 ETDZs were launched, including Dalian, Qinhuangdao, Tianjin, Yantai, Qingdao, Lianyungang, Nantong, Minhang, Hongqiao, Caohejing, Ningbo, Fuzhou, Guangzhou, and Zhanjiang.[95] While these ETDZs tended to be relatively smaller suburban areas than SEZs, they also enjoyed preferential tax treatment in order to enhance investment environment and encourage industrial projects in the high-tech industry.[96] Two more waves of substantial growth in ETDZs took place around 1991 to 1992 and 2000 to 2002. In 2003 the realized inward FDI in these zones amounted to $15.769 billion.[97] As of 2016, 54 state-level ETDZs existed in China, with 32 in coastal regions and 22 in the hinterland.[98]

To level up the productivity of the SEZs and ETDZs, ICT infrastructure building became a priority. In pursuit of capital formation and network upgrades, China's government was first and foremost concerned with "linking coastal cities and responding to the demand of businesses" for the outward-looking economy, and, according to Yu Hong, the telecom infrastructure and communication facilities in Guangdong were much better versed than the inland provinces like Hunan and Sichuan.[99]

These elements advanced the social-economic conditions in coastal areas that gave birth to numerous technology companies. Taking Shenzhen as an example, the share of high-tech industries in its total industrial output increased from less than 10 percent in 1990 to nearly 40 percent in 1998.[100] Some saw Shenzhen city as China's Silicon Valley: in 2014 alone Shenzhen hosted a total of $10.42 billion (RMB 64 billion) in investment in research and development (R&D).[101] Apart from foreign-funded or established technology companies, some well-known domestically launched firms grew here, including the global telecommunications equipment leaders ZTE, founded in 1985; Huawei, founded in 1987; and the Internet giant Tencent.

The Workforce

A second aspect of the massive industrialization and urbanization was the rise of an urban working class, as "the growing ICT sector has become a major destination for millions of peasants-cum-workers."[102] According to MII's documentation, about 6.2 million people were working in the electronic information industry in 2002, up from 1.5 million five years before; 16 million workers (6.7 percent of the urban employment) were employed in the broadly defined ICT industry.[103]

In a more general sense, an even larger population formed what Jack Linchuan Qiu called the "information-have-less": 247 million migrant workers as of 2015, 114 million manufacturing workers as of 2013, 227 million people under four years of age and 222 million people 60 years old and older.[104] These people were the primary users of less expensive, more accessible, and low-end ICTs, such as "second-hand phones, used computers, pirated DVDs, Internet cafes, short-message service (SMS), prepaid mobile service, and the Little Smart low-end wireless phone."[105] These populations would become active users of many of Tencent's popular products, such as QQ, WeChat, and mini-games, among others, discussed in later chapters.

The Birth of Tencent

Founded in 1998, Tencent started the business with an instant messaging (IM) service—QQ. QQ, developed by Tencent's five core founders—Ma Huateng, Zeng Liqing, Zhang Zhidon, Chen Yidan, and Xu Chenye—was a localized adaptation of ICQ, an instant messenger an Israeli company originally invented.[106] Tencent has been working continually on adding Chinese features to this instant messenger system ever since. The wide popularity of QQ won Tencent a large user base in China. By the end of 2018, QQ's monthly active users (MAU) reached 807 million.[107] Thanks partly to such a gigantic user base, as will be shown, Tencent's businesses have expanded to a variety of other value-added Internet, mobile, and telecom services. Value-added services (VAS) are generally defined as "enhanced data-processing services" beyond the basic voice services ordinarily provided by telecommunications carriers.[108] In China, the State Council promulgated the Telecommunications Regulations of the People's Republic of China first in 2000 in which the differences between the basic and the VAS were specified:

> Telecommunications businesses shall be divided into the categories of basic telecommunications businesses and value-added telecommunications businesses. . . . Basic telecommunications businesses shall mean businesses that provide public network infrastructure, services for public data transmission and basic voice telephony services. Value-added telecommunications businesses shall mean businesses that provide telecommunications and information services using public network infrastructure.[109]

In the case of Tencent, its VASs include entertainment, social networking, communication and information portal, gaming, and e-commerce, among others, on smart mobile handsets and the home devices.[110] In June 2004 Tencent launched an initial public offering (IPO) of shares on the Hong

Kong Stock Exchange. At the end of 2018, its revenue topped $45.56 billion (RMB 312.69 billion).[111] The company, identifying itself as an "online lifestyle services provider," claims to be "China's largest and most used Internet service portal."[112] Tencent is currently among the top ten largest Internet conglomerates worldwide in terms of market value.[113]

Tencent was founded at a critical point to both Chinese and global Internet industries. On the domestic side, Deng embarked on his second southern tour in 1992 during which he firmly advocated further reform and more economic liberalization.[114] This speech carried far-reaching historical significance for China's economic development, as Deng's famous statement, "Be it a black cat or a white cat, a cat that can catch mice is a good cat," was generally recognized as an open and welcoming attitude to the capitalist market.[115] Shenzhen, where Tencent's headquarters is based, greatly benefited from Deng's visit and became one of China's earliest SEZs that opened up to foreign capital after 1992.[116] In just one year after Deng's visit, the amount of FDI into Shenzhen rose from $250 million in 1992 to $497 million in 1993. In 2009 the amount of FDI in Shenzhen reached $4.2 billion.[117] The per capita GDP in Shenzhen increased from $1,825 (RMB 8,720) in 1990 to $8,713 (RMB 69,450) in 2006, and GDP was growing at a rate of 14 to 20 percent a year between 1995 and 2006.[118] At the same time, Shenzhen was among the first few cities in China to have Internet access via China Telecom, after the first full Internet operation using the TCP/IP protocol in China was launched in 1994.[119] The following years saw Internet companies springing up all over China, particularly in Shenzhen. On the global side, at the same time, ICTs were becoming booming industries for the economy in the United States. Particularly, this was evident in the rise of the NASDAQ, where a growing number of technology companies were publicly listed. Tencent, emerging in the concluding years of the 20th century, is one example of this global Internet gold rush.

Conclusion

This chapter provides a review of the political-economy context within which China's ICT industry and, more specifically, Tencent grew. As the four stages of major changes in policy guidelines and articulation delineate, these shifts were not incidental. They were both the preconditions and outcomes of the overall political-economic transformation that took place in China's contemporary history. The evolution of the Internet from a network infrastructure that facilitated industrial development to a central node of national economy itself reflected a broad political-economic transformation from an outward-looking production mode that was heavily dependent on FDIs in manufacturing to a domestically centered and consumption-driven mode with the support from portfolio investments.[120]

While these changes and developments were highly government initiated, they represented a more general pattern in the world, where private capital—whether domestic or foreign—was unleashed to build a country's economy. China was the leading example of this pattern. Based on the experience of other countries, China's leaders sought to gradually open up the domestic market to foreign investors as well as to domestic private companies. At the same time, this process also displayed some Chinese characteristics—the restrictions on FDI in certain areas. A result of the restrictions was an extensive incorporation of foreign venture-capital investments in the Internet industry, which is further discussed in following chapters on Tencent's capital structure. In other words, Chinese Internet policies had always made room for capital development, yet they were continually adjusted in terms of room for whom and development of which unit of capital—if it was state-owned or private-owned and if it was domestic or foreign.

These changes responded to both internal and external challenges and demonstrated an intertwined relation between the Chinese state and various units of capital. On the domestic side, a growing Internet industry could be attributed to several factors, including the elevation of private capital, the participation of domestic and foreign units of capital, a spatial shift in the allocations of the great labor army, and policy preferences given to the information technology sector. Internationally, foreign investors' desires to enter the Chinese market, the rise of a global financial sector, the collaboration with the rising power of Silicon Valley, and the crisis and depression of the latest years also contributed to the Internet boom in China at different stages. The negotiations, collaborations, and competitions among different state sectors and units of capital have been ongoing.

Notes

1. Milton L. Mueller and Zixiang Tan, *China: Telecommunications and the Dilemmas of Reform* (Westport, CT: Praeger, 1997), 83; "The Internet Timeline of China 1986~2003," *CNNIC*, n.d., accessed May 10, 2016, http://www1.cnnic.cn/IDR/hlwfzdsj/201306/t20130628_40563.htm.
2. "Internet Timeline of China 1986~2003."
3. "The Annual Statistical Report on Internet Development in China, 1997 and 2000," *CNNIC*, n.d., accessed October 10, 2016, www.cnnic.net.cn/hlwfzyj/hlwxzbg/200905/P020120709345374625930.pdf and www.cnnic.net.cn/hlwfzyj/hlwxzbg/200905/P020120709345371437524.pdf.
4. Arjun Kharpal, "Alibaba Sets New Singles Day Record with More Than $30.8 Billion in Sales in 24 Hours," *CNBC*, November 11, 2018, accessed January 9, 2019, www.cnbc.com/2018/11/11/alibaba-singles-day-2018-record-sales-on-largest-shopping-event-day.html.
5. Nina Hachgian, "China's Cyber-Strategy," *Foreign Affairs* (March–April 2001): 118–33.
6. Wenli Yuan, "E-Democracy@China: Does It Work?" *Chinese Journal of Communication* 3, no. 4 (2010): 488–503.

7. Sally J. McMillan and Jang-sun Hwang, "Nailing Jell-O to the Wall and Herding Cats: A Content Analysis of Chinese and U.S. Newspaper Coverage of the Internet in China," *Journal of Intercultural Communication Research* 31, no. 2 (2002): 107.
8. Yuan, "E-Democracy@China."
9. McChesney, *Communication Revolution*, 14.
10. Vincent Mosco, "Toward a Theory of the State and Telecommunications Policy," *Journal of Communication* 38, no. 1 (1988): 107–24.
11. Yuezhi Zhao, *Communication in China: Political Economy, Power, and Conflict* (Lanham, MD: Rowman & Littlefield, 2008), 20–21.
12. Leo A. Orleans, *Science in Contemporary China* (Stanford: Stanford University Press, 1980), 535–40.
13. "Deng Xiaoping's South China Tour (Jan. 1992)," *China.org.cn*, April 19, 2011, accessed February 24, 2019, www.china.org.cn/china/CPC_90_anniversary/2011-04/19/content_22392494.htm.
14. Chengzhong Guo, "Zhongguo Xinxihua fazhan lichen he jiben silu" 中国信息化发展历程和基本思路 [The Path and Guideline of China's Informatization], n.p., accessed May 11, 2016, www.ccidnet.com/2002/0731/20953.shtml.
15. "Across the Great Wall: Celebration, First Email Message from China to CSNET," *Amateur Computerist* 16, no. 2 (2008), accessed May 10, 2016, www.columbia.edu/~hauben/acn/ACn16-2.pdf.
16. Cindy Zheng, "Opening the Digital Door: Computer Networking in China," *Telecommunications Policy* 18, no. 3 (1994): 236–42.
17. Mueller and Tan, *China in the Information Age*, 83.
18. "Across the Great Wall"; "Internet Timeline of China 1986~2003."
19. "Internet Timeline of China 1986~2003."
20. Mueller and Tan, *China in the Information Age*, 84.
21. Wei Wu, "Great Leap or Long March: Some Policy Issues of the Development of the Internet in China," *Telecommunications Policy* 20, no. 9 (1996): 699–711.
22. "Internet Timeline of China 1986~2003"; W. Wu, "Great Leap"; Mueller and Tan, *China in the Information Age*, 85.
23. "Internet Timeline of China 1986~2003."
24. W. Wu, "Great Leap."
25. "Internet Timeline of China 1986~2003."
26. Ding Lu, "China's Telecommunications Infrastructure Buildup: On Its Own Way," in *Deregulation and Interdependence in the Asia-Pacific Region*, eds. Takatoshi Ito and Anne O. Krueger (Chicago: University of Chicago Press, 2000), 371–413.
27. W. Wu, "Great Leap"; "Internet Timeline of China 1986~2003."
28. Mueller and Tan, *China in the Information Age*, 87.
29. Zixiang (Alex) Tan, William Foster, and Seymour Goodman, "China's State-Coordinated Internet Infrastructure," *Communications of the ACM* 42, no. 6 (1999): 44–52.
30. Peter Lovelock, Theodore C. Clark, and Ben A. Petrazzini. "The 'Golden Projects': China's National Networking Initiative," *Information Infrastructure and Policy* 5, no. 4 (1996): 265.
31. "Internet Timeline of China 1986–2003."
32. Lovelock, Clark, and Petrazzini, "Golden Projects," 265–77.
33. Mueller and Tan, *China in the Information Age*, 52, 57.
34. Lovelock, Clark, and Petrazzini, "Golden Projects," 265–77.
35. W. Wu, "Great Leap"; Mueller and Tan, *China in the Information Age*, 91.
36. Mueller and Tan, *China in the Information Age*, 91.

37. Bryce T. McIntyre, "Let a Hundred Modems Bloom: The Internet in Today's China," in *Cyberpath to Development in Asia: Issues and Challenges*, eds. Sandhya Rao and Bruce C. Klopfenstein (Westport, CT: Praeger, 2002), 71–72.
38. Mueller and Tan, *China in the Information Age*, 91.
39. W. Wu, "Great Leap."
40. "Ninth Five-Year Plan (1996–2000) for National Economic and Social Development and Long-Range Objectives to the Year 2010," *State Council*, n.d., accessed April 4, 2016, http://cpc.people.com.cn/GB/64184/64186/66686/4494253.html.
41. Li Peng, "Report on the Outline of the Ninth Five-Year Plan (1996–2000) for National Economic and Social Development and the Long-Range Objectives to the Year 2010 (Excerpts)," *Ninth Five-Year Plan in Retrospect*, accessed November 4, 2016, www.china.org.cn/95e/95-english1/2.htm.
42. "Ninth Five-Year Plan (1996–2000)"; S. Philip Hsu, Yu-Shan Wu, and Suisheng Zhao, eds., *In Search of China's Development Model: Beyond the Beijing Consensus* (London: Routledge, 2011), 138.
43. Shi Zhong-Liang, "Outline of the Ninth Five-Year Plan for National Economic and Social Development and the Long-Term Goals to the Year 2010," in *China's Transition to a Socialist Market Economy*, ed. Mohamed Osman Suliman (Westport, CT: Quorum, 1998), 128.
44. Li, "Report on the Outline of the Ninth Five-Year Plan."
45. John Wong, *The Political Economy of Deng's Nanxun: Breakthrough in China's Reform and Development* (Hackensack, NJ: World Scientific, 2014), 92–94.
46. Qian Zeng, "Zhongguo Hulianwang jiandu zhengce fenxi (1994–2014): Yizhong kaifaxing weiquan zhuyi" 中国互联网监督政策分析（1994–2014）:一种开发型威权主义 [Analysis on Chinese Internet Regulation Policies (1994–2014): A Developmental Authoritarianism], in *Legalization of Cyberspace: Annual Report of Internet and State Governance 2015*, ed. Zhian Zhang (Beijing: Commercial, 2015), 160–70.
47. "China's Technological Progress," *People's Daily*, October 8, 2000, accessed November 4, 2016, www.china.org.cn/95e/95-english3/15.htm.
48. "China's IT Develops at Tremendous Pace," *People's Daily*, September 25, 2000, accessed November 4, 2016, www.china.org.cn/95e/95-english3/3.htm; Unless otherwise noted, this and subsequent calculations of RMB to USD currency, exchange rates are derived from "Official Exchange Rate (LCU per US$, Period Average)," *World Bank*, accessed November 4, 2016, http://data.worldbank.org/indicator/PA.NUS.FCRF?end=2015&locations=CN&start=1960&view=chart.
49. "Investments Pave Way for Growth," *China Daily*, October 3, 2000, accessed November 4, 2016, www.china.org.cn/95e/95-english2/17.htm.
50. Yukai Wang, "Zhongyang Wangluo anquan yu xinxihua lingdao xiaozu de youlai ji yingxiang" 中央网络安全与信息化领导小组的由来及其影响 [The Origin and Influence of the Central Leading Group for Cyberspace Affairs and the Cyberspace Administration of China], March 3, 2014, accessed May 11, 2016, http://theory.people.com.cn/n/2014/0303/c40531-24510897.html; "Internet Timeline of China 1986~2003."
51. "Internet Timeline of China 1986~2003"; "State Council, Circular of the General Office of the State Council Concerning Establishing Information Work Leading Group of the State Council," n.d., accessed July 30, 2016, www.chinabaike.com/law/zy/xz/bgt/1335454.html.
52. "State Council, Circular of the General Office of the State Council Concerning Establishing National Information Work Leading Group," n.d., accessed July 30, 2016, www.gov.cn/gongbao/content/2000/content_60619.htm.

53. "Zhongyang Wangluo Anquan he Xinxihua lingdao xiaozu chengli" 中央网络安全和信息化领导小组成立 [The Central Leading Group for Cyberspace Affairs and the Cyberspace Administration of China Is Established], *Xinhua News*, February 28, 2014, accessed July 30, 2016, http://news.xinhuanet.com/info/2014-02/28/c_133148759.htm; "China Eyes Internet Power," *Xinhua News*, March 8, 2014, accessed July 30, 2016, http://news.xinhuanet.com/english/special/2014-03/08/c_133171308.htm.
54. Y. Wang, "Origin and Influence of the Central Leading Group"; "China Eyes Internet Power."
55. Mueller and Tan, *China in the Information Age*, 24–25.
56. Eric Harwit and Jack Su, "A Telecom Newcomer Challenges the MPT Monopoly," *China Business Review* 23, no. 6 (1996): 22–23.
57. Mueller and Tan, *China in the Information Age*, 52.
58. Explanation for State Council's Ministerial Reform, n.d., accessed July 30, 2016, www.reformdata.org/content/19980306/12912.html.
59. Dali L. Yang, *Remaking the Chinese Leviathan: Market Transition and the Politics of Governance in China* (Stanford: Stanford University Press, 2004), 17–19.
60. "Ministry of Industry and Information Technology Inaugurated," *Xinhua News Agency*, June 30, 2008, accessed November 10, 2016, www.china.org.cn/government/news/2008-06/30/content_15906787.htm.
61. Yukyung Yeo, "Remaking the Chinese State and the Nature of Economic Governance? The Early Appraisal of the 2008 'Super-Ministry' Reform," *Journal of Contemporary China* 18, no. 62 (2009): 729–43.
62. "The Eleventh Five-Year Plan for Information Industry," *MIIT*, March 2, 2007.
63. "The Twelfth Five-Year Plan Will Invest 2 Trillion in Telecommunications Industry," *MIIT*, December 23, 2010, accessed November 10, 2016, www.cn-c114.net/575/a571178.html.
64. "2010 nian Dianxi xinxi chanye tongji gongbao" 2010年电子信息产业统计公报 [The 2010 Statistical Report of Electrical Information Industry], *MIIT*, February 11, 2011, accessed November 10, 2016, www.miit.gov.cn/n1146312/n1146904/n1648373/c3483292/content.html.
65. "China: Summary of the Tenth Five-Year Plan (2001–2005)—Information Industry," accessed November 10, 2016, http://unpan1.un.org/intradoc/groups/public/documents/apcity/unpan022769.pdf.
66. Harvey, *Brief History*, 121–25.
67. Justin Yifu Lin, "China and the Global Economy," paper presented at Asia Economic Policy Conference, November 29–30, 2011, accessed November 10, 2016, https://www.frbsf.org/economic-research/files/Lin.pdf; World Bank National Accounts Data, "Exports of Goods and Services (% of GDP)," *World Bank*, n.d., accessed November 10, 2016, http://data.worldbank.org/indicator/NE.EXP.GNFS.ZS?locations=CN.
68. John Bellamy Foster and Robert W. McChesney, *The Endless Crisis: How Monopoly-Finance Capital Produces Stagnation and Upheaval from the USA to China* (New York: Monthly Review, 2012), 169.
69. Yuezhi Zhao, "China's Pursuits of Indigenous Innovations in Information Technology Developments: Hopes, Follies and Uncertainties," *Chinese Journal of Communication* 3, no. 3 (2010): 266–89.
70. Yuezhi Zhao, "Neoliberal Strategies, Socialism Legacies: Communication and State Transformation in China," in *Global Communication: Toward a Transcultural Political Economy*, eds. Paula Chakravartty and Yuezhi Zhao (Lanham, MD: Rowman & Littlefield, 2008), 23–50.

71. Hong, "Reading the Twelfth Five-Year Plan."
72. Ibid.
73. "China's Internet Developments During the 12th Five-Year Plan," *State Council*, November 4, 2015, accessed November 10, 2016, http://english.gov.cn/policies/infographics/2015/11/04/content_281475227710554.htm.
74. Ibid.
75. "Statistical Report on Internet Development in China," *CNNIC*, 2018.
76. Li Keqiang, "Report on the Work of the Government 2015," speech delivered at the Third Session of the 12th National People' s Congress, March 5, 2015, accessed July 1, 2015, http://news.xinhuanet.com/english/china/2015-03/16/c_134071473_2.htm.
77. Benfu Lu and Junlan Zhou, "Gongxiang jingji de chuangye dachao he shangye moshi fenxi" 共享经济的创业大潮和商业模式分析 [An analysis on the Sharing Economy and Its Business Model],in *Legalization of Cyberspace: Annual Report of Internet and State Governance 2015* (Beijing: Commercial, 2015), 127–36; Guomin Yu, "Hulianwang shi gaowei meijie: Yizhong shehui chuanbo gouzao de quanxin fanshi—Guanyu xianjieduan chuanmei fazhan ruogan lilun yu shijian wenti de bianzheng" 互联网是高维媒介：一种社会传播构造的全新范式—关于现阶段传媒发展若干理论与实践问题的辩证 [Internet Is High-Dimensional Media: A Brand-New Paradigm of Social Communication Construction—A Dialectical View of Current Theory and Practice], in *Legalization of Cyberspace: Annual Report of Internet and State Governance 2015*, ed. Zhian Zhang (Beijing: Commercial, 2015), 209–17.
78. "Instruction on Actively Promoting 'Internet-Plus' Strategy," *State Council*, July 4, 2015, accessed April 4, 2016, www.gov.cn/zhengce/content/2015-07/04/content_10002.htm; Hong, *Networking China*, 133.
79. Mueller and Tan, *China in the Information Age*, 1–3.
80. Q. Zeng, "Zhongguo Hulianwang jiandu zhengce fenxi (1994–2014)," 160–70.
81. Edward Tse, *China's Disruptors: How Alibaba, Xiaomi, Tencent, and Other Companies Are Changing the Rules of Business* (New York: Portfolio, 2015), x–xi.
82. Nicholas R. Lardy, *Markets Over Mao: The Rise of Private Business in China* (Washington, DC: Peterson Institute for International Economics, 2014), 64.
83. Ibid., 62–63.
84. Ibid., 66.
85. Ibid., 87.
86. Heng-Hao Chang and Alvin Y. So, "Powerful Communist Party, Robust Capitalist Economy: Interpreting the Chinese Puzzle," *Humboldt Journal of Social Relations* 24, no. 1–2 (1998): 101–27; Andrew Atherton and Alaric Fairbanks, "Stimulating Private Sector Development in China: The Emergence of Enterprise Development Centres in Liaoning and Sichuan Provinces," *Asia Pacific Business Review* 12, no. 3 (2006): 333–54.
87. Mohamed Jalloh, "Jack Ma: Success Story," *Investopedia*, n.d., accessed November 8, 2016, www.investopedia.com/university/jack-ma-biography/jack-ma-success-story.asp; "Zhongwang baojing cangsang jiehou yusheng Wanpingguo huishou jianxin lichen" 中网饱经沧桑劫后余生 万平国回首艰辛历程 [The Survival of Chinanet and Wan Pingguo's Reflection], *Caijing Shibao* 财经时报, July 12, 2001, accessed November 8, 2016, http://tech.sina.com.cn/i/c/75586.shtml; "Zhangshuxin: Yinghaiwei dangnian shibai, shi yinwei ta taizao le" 张树新：瀛海威当年失败，是因为"它太早了" [Zhang Shuxin: The Failure of Yinghaiwei Was Due to Its Early Appearance], *Tai Meiti* 钛媒体, April 21, 2014, accessed November 8, 2016, http://tech.163.com/14/0421/08/9QBFA1S400094ODU.html; Jun Lin, *Feiteng Shiwu nian: China's Internet 1995–2009* 沸腾十五年：中国互

联网*1995–2009 [The Hustle and Bustle of China's Internet: Fifteen Years Between 1995–2009]* (Beijing: China Citic, 2009), 1–27.
88. Lin, *Feiteng Shiwu nian: China's Internet 1995–2009*; Tse, *China's Disruptors*.
89. Mianmian Zhang, "2016 Zhongguo Hulianwang qiye 100 qiang paihangbang fabu" 2016中国互联网企业100强排行榜发布 [The Top 100 Chinese Internet companies in 2016], *Yangguang Wang* 央广网, July 15, 2016, accessed November 8, 2016, www.cbdio.com/BigData/2016-07/15/content_5090837.htm.
90. "1979 nian 7 yue 15 ri Zhonggong Zhongyang Guowu Yuan jueding dui Guangdong Fujian liangsheng duiwai jingji geiyu gengduo zizhu quan" 1979年7月15日 中共中央、国务院决定对广东、福建两省对外经济给以更多自主权 [The Central Committee of the Communist Party of China and the State Council Decided to Give More Autonomy to Guangdong and Fujian Provinces in Foreign Economic Relations on July 15, 1979], *People.com.cn*, accessed November 15, 2016, http://cpc.people.com.cn/GB/4162/64165/67447/67829/4590607.html; Yue-man Yeung, Joanna Lee, and Gordon Kee, "China's Special Economic Zones at 30," *Eurasian Geography and Economics* 50, no. 2 (2009): 222–40.
91. "Shiban Jingji tequ de juece neiqing Weihe Guangdong Fujian xianzou yibu" 试办经济特区的决策内情 为何广东、福建先走一步 [An Insider View of Why Guangdong and Fujian Were the First Provinces for Special Economic Zone Experiments], *Dangshi Bolan* 党史博览, 6 (2008), accessed November 15, 2016, http://cpc.people.com.cn/GB/68742/69118/69658/7433454.html.
92. "Regulations on Special Economic Zones in Guangdong Province," Fifteenth Meeting of the Standing Committee of the Fifth National People's Congress, August 26, 1980, accessed November 15, 2016, www.wto.org/english/thewto_e/acc_e/chn_e/WTACCCHN46_LEG_8.pdf.
93. Yeung, Lee, and Kee, "China's Special Economic Zones at 30."
94. Kwan-Yiu Wong, "China's Special Economic Zone Experiment: An Appraisal," Series B, Human Geography, *Geografiska Annaler* 69, no. 1 (1987): 27–40.
95. "A Brief Introduction of National Economic and Technological Development Zones in China," *Ministry of Commerce*, accessed November 15, 2016, www.china.org.cn/english/SPORT-c/76751.htm.
96. "Tax Policies Concerning Foreign-funded Enterprises and Foreign Enterprises in National ETDZs," *Ministry of Commerce*, accessed November 15, 2016, www.china.org.cn/english/difang/76259.htm.
97. Bih Jane Liu and Yu-Yin Wu, "Development Zones in China: Are STIPs a Substitute for or a Complement to ETDZs?" *Taipei Economic Inquiry* 47, no. 1 (2011): 97–145.
98. "Introduction to China Industrial Parks," *China Knowledge*, accessed November 15, 2016, www.chinaknowledge.com/Manufacturing/Introduction.aspx?subchap=3&content=7.
99. Yu Hong, "Repurposing Telecoms for Capital in China," *Asian Survey* 53, no. 2 (2013): 319–47.
100. Xie Wei, "Acquisition of Technological Capability Through Special Economic Zones (SEZs): The Case of Shenzhen SEZ," *Industry and Innovation* 7, no. 2 (2000): 199–221.
101. He Huifeng, "Top 5 Tech Giants Who Shape Shenzhen, 'China's Silicon Valley,'" *South China Morning Post*, April 17, 2015, accessed November 15, 2016, www.scmp.com/lifestyle/technology/enterprises/article/1765430/top-5-tech-giants-who-shape-shenzhen-chinas-silicon.
102. Hong, *Labor, Class Formation*, 6.
103. Ibid. Min Wen and Weihua Deng, "Xinxi chanye bu: Woguo xinxi chanye jinru xinyilun jiegou tiaozheng qi" 信息产业部：我国信息产业进入新一轮结构调整期 [The Ministry of Information Industry: The Nation Enters a

New Round of Structural Adjustment in Information Industry], *Xinhua News*, October 21, 2002, accessed November 15, 2016, http://news.xinhuanet.com/zhengfu/2002-10/21/content_603505.htm.

104. "Guojia weisheng jisheng wei zhongguo liudong renkou fazhan baogao (2016) deng youguan qingkuang zhuanti fabu hui weizi shilu" 国家卫生计生委中国流动人口发展报告 (2016) 等有关情况专题发布会文字实录 [Text Report of 2016 Press Conference on Chinese Migrant Populations by National Health and Family Planning Commission], *National Health and Family Planning Commission*, October 19, 2016, accessed November 15, 2016, www.nhfpc.gov.cn/xcs/s3574/201610/a6d3a604596a4ca3acf0dad31d891c13.shtml; Richard A. McCormack, "By the Numbers: The U.S. Has 12 Million Manufacturing Workers; China Has Ten Times That Number—114 Million," *Manufacturing and Technology News* 23, no. 6 (2016), accessed November 15, 2016, www.manufacturingnews.com/news/2016/China-Manufacturing-Employment-0630161.html; "2015 nian Quanguo 1% renkou chouyang diaocha zhuyao shuju gongbao" 2015 年全国1%人口抽样调查主要数据公报 [China 1% Population Sample Survey in 2015], *National Bureau of Statistics*, April 20, 2016, accessed November 15, 2016, www.stats.gov.cn/tjsj/zxfb/201604/t20160420_1346151.html; Jack Linchuan Qiu, *Working-Class Network Society: Communication Technology and the Information Have-Less in Urban China* (Cambridge, MA: MIT Press), 85–87.
105. Qiu, *Working-Class Network Society*, 3.
106. ICQ was later bought by AOL and now is owned by Mail.ru.
107. Tencent, "Tencent Announces 2018 Fourth Quarter and Annual Results," March 21, 2019, accessed March 25, 2019, www.tencent.com/en-us/articles/15000761553167321.pdf.
108. Milton L. Mueller and Wolter Lemstra, "Liberalization and the Internet," in *International Handbook of Network Industries: The Liberalization of Infrastructure*, eds. Matthias Finger and Rolf W. Kunneke (Cheltenham: Elgar, 2011), 144–61.
109. State Council, "Telecommunications Regulations of the People's Republic of China," *ChinaITLaw.org*, January 20, 2010, accessed April 23, 2017, www.china.org.cn/business/laws_regulations/2010-01/20/content_19273945_2.htm.
110. Tencent, Prospectus, 2004, 58.
111. Tencent, "Tencent Announces 2018 Fourth Quarter and Annual Results."
112. "About Tencent," *Tencent*, n.d., accessed July 20, 2015, www.tencent.com/en-us/abouttencent.html.
113. "Market Capitalization of the Biggest Internet Companies Worldwide as of May 2018 (in Billion U.S. Dollars)," *Statista*, accessed January 17, 2019, www.statista.com/statistics/277483/market-value-of-the-largest-internet-companies-worldwide/.
114. Suisheng Zhao, "Deng Xiaoping's Southern Tour: Elite Politics in Post-Tiananmen China," *Asian Survey* 33, no. 8 (1993): 739–56.
115. "Southern Tour Legacy," *Global Times*, n.d., accessed July 20, 2015, http://backup.globaltimes.cn/specialcoverage/dengssoutherntour.aspx.
116. Lin Huang, "What Did Deng Xiaoping's Southern Tour Bring to Shenzhen?" *Party History*, n.d., accessed July 20, 2015, http://dangshi.people.com.cn/BIG5/18156136.html.
117. Xiangming Chen and Ahmed Kanna, *Rethinking Global Urbanism: Comparative Insights from Secondary Cities* (New York: Routledge, 2012), 112–13.
118. Jianfa Shen, "Urban Growth and Sustainable Development in Shenzhen City 1980–2006," *Open Environmental Journal* 2 (2008): 71–79.
119. Mueller and Tan, *China in the Information Age*, 81–82.
120. Hong, "Reading the Twelfth Five-Year Plan," 1045–57.

2 Economic Profile

Founded in 1998, Tencent now is the seventh largest Internet company in the world, with a market capitalization of over $400 billion. As the company celebrated its 20th anniversary in 2018, Tencent announced a strategic corporate reorganization and upgrade, aiming at better serving enterprise and industrial clients through "the convergence of social, content, and technology trends." Proudly proclaiming itself an "online lifestyle service" provider, Tencent said it had "brought together China's largest Internet community."[1]

But, what are the scope and reach of Tencent's businesses? How are its business and finance structured to make the company competitive in so many different areas? What factors contribute to Tencent's success in China's Internet industry? These are not just business school "101" type of questions that seek to understand marketing strategies, consumer behaviors, or managing skills but are critical political-economic ones that allow exploration of Tencent as a site of interactions among units of capital within the web of a national and transnational Internet industry.

Some studies touch upon the commercial aspects of Tencent. Haibo Zou discusses how Tencent utilized the network effect aggregated by the massive adoption of QQ to promote other pay services.[2] Junjie Zhang argues that Tencent's successful transformation from a single business to diversifications builds on the network of instant communication.[3] More recent studies look into its flagship product Weixin and WeChat.[4] Shijie Wang examines the micromarketing strategies on Weixin and WeChat, which took advantage of users' social networks and location-based information.[5] A limited number of studies published in English focus on Tencent's business strategies as an example for the digital industry.[6] While these studies contributed to understanding Tencent's profit-making mechanisms on micro levels, they did not present an institutional context within which Tencent develops.

This chapter analyzes the basic economic features of Tencent through examining the reach of its business activities and the scope of its product lines. Explored are the broad range and extent of Tencent's value-added, Internet-related services and the courses of integration and diversification as the company collaborates with other domestic units of Internet capital. Tencent has displayed the intrinsic trends of capital reproduction and expansion in forms of horizontal integration, vertical integration, and diversification. Equally important is the company's strategic choices in its acquisitions, mergers, and partnerships, as its achievement largely depends on a number of successful alliances with several leading Internet companies and thus mirrors the inter-capital relations in China.

Corporate Structure and Financial Performance

Tencent was founded in November 1998 as Shenzhen Tencent Computer Systems Co. Ltd.[7] The five core founders were Ma Huateng, Zhang Zhidong, Xu Chenye, Chen Yidan, and Zeng Liqing. Four of them—Ma, Zhang, Xu, and Chen—were schoolmates and friends who knew each other from middle school and college. Zeng and Ma's sister were colleagues at Shenzhen Telecom. At Tencent, Zeng was in charge of sales and marketing; the other four were primarily focusing on developing computer programs and products. The government's requirement for registered capital to start a company was $60,386 (RMB 500,000) back then. These five young men put together their own savings, and each contributed a portion to the seed funding.

The company initially, like many in the infant stage, did not have a clear direction until it started developing an instant messaging system (IM). IM comprised a unique communication format, and it predated the concept of real-time interactive conversation; an early successful prototype came in 1996 when the Israeli company Mirabilis launched the software ICQ.[8] In June 1998, with already 21 million users, Mirabilis was acquired by America Online (AOL), the then U.S. Internet giant; in August 1998 Tencent brought ICQ to China with the name OICQ.[9]

In the late 1990s personal computers and household Internet were not widely accessible in China due to their high cost. Urban working classes

Table 2.1 Registered Capital of Original Shareholders

Stockholder	*Investment (RMB)*	*Percentage*
Ma Huateng	237,500	47.5
Zhang Zhidong	100,000	20.0
Zeng Liqing	62,500	12.5
Xu Chenye	50,000	10.0
Chen Yidan	50,000	10.0

Source: Lin and Zhang, *Ma Huateng's Tencent Empire*, 33–34.

mostly went to Internet cafes and net bars—where the owners maintained dozens of computer terminals, paid the Internet service providers (ISP), and charged users based on the time they spent online—for online activities.[10] In such an environment, connection speed and security of personal information were users' primary concerns. Tencent improved OICQ by compressing the size of the software package so that users could download it quickly and store their contacts in their online accounts instead of on the shared computers in Internet cafes. OICQ was officially launched in February 1999, making Tencent one of the first IM providers in China.[11] Within half a year, registered users reached one million.[12] This laid the foundation for its future success in Internet and mobile value-added services.

On November 23, 1999, Tencent incorporated another company, this time in the British Virgin Islands under the name of Keyword Technology Ltd. This later became the parent company of the Tencent group—Tencent Holdings Ltd. In 2004, before its initial public offering, Tencent changed its registration location to the Cayman Islands and its name to Tencent Holdings Ltd.[13] To register an offshore parent company was not uncommon among Chinese Internet companies because of the easy registration process, low maintenance cost, and low tax in the British Cayman Islands.[14]

In February 2000 Tencent established a wholly owned subsidiary company, Tencent Technology (Shenzhen) Co. Ltd.[15] The aim was to separate its businesses in software development and value-added services (VAS) to different subsidiary companies so that the company would be able to incorporate foreign investments while running the value-added telecommunications and Internet services.

Tencent's IM business continued to grow in 2000. By April 2000, registered accounts of OICQ reached five million.[16] To promote its brand, Tencent designed a cartoon-penguin icon, which immediately became the symbol of the company.[17] However, AOL accused OICQ of violating the intellectual property rights of ICQ.[18] In December 2000 Tencent changed the name of its IM service into QQ.[19]

Also in 2000, Tencent started collaborating with China Unicom and China Mobile's Guangdong Bureaus as both telecom giants launched their first wireless application protocol (WAP) services and agreed to include mobile QQ as a preinstalled program in their newly issued SIM cards.[20] Shortly after, Tencent started working with the local bureaus of China Mobile in Beijing, Sichuan, Jiangsu, Zhejiang, and Shanxi, among others.[21] By 2004 Tencent was working with 44 subsidiaries and branches of China Mobile and China Unicom in delivering its mobile and telecommunications VAS.[22] The diffusion of the mobile Internet contributed hugely to Tencent's balance sheet:

> For the year ended December 31, 2003, our revenues and profit for the year were RMB 735.0 million [US$ 88.88 million] and RMB 322.2 million [US$ 38.96 million], respectively, representing an annual growth rate of 179.4 percent and 129.0 percent from 2002, respectively. Subscription-based revenues accounted for over 75 percent of our total revenues in 2003. For the three months ended March 31, 2004, our revenues and profit for the period were RMB 257.6 million [US$ 31.25] and RMB 107.3 million [US$ 12.97], respectively.[23]

In the meantime, Tencent further integrated its corporate framework in prospect of an IPO. In early 2004 Tencent established two more subsidiaries: Shenzhen Shiji Kaixuan Technology Co. Ltd. (Shiji Kaixuan) and Shidai Zhaoyang Technology (Shenzhen) Co. Ltd. (Shidai Zhaoyang). Shiji Kaixuan Technology, incorporated as a private limited company, was designed to provide Internet and telecommunication VAS similar to Tencent Computer.[24] Shidai Zhaoyang was registered as a wholly foreign owned entity running software businesses like Tencent Technology.[25]

On June 16, 2004, after nearly one year's preparation, Tencent was publicly listed on Hong Kong Stock Exchange (HKSE).[26] Tencent enlisted Goldman Sachs as its "global coordinator, lead manager and bookrunner of the offering" in 2003.[27] According to Tencent, the collaboration between Tencent and Goldman Sachs was the result of "mutual respect and appreciation."[28] In fact, at the time, Goldman Sachs was the leading underwriter

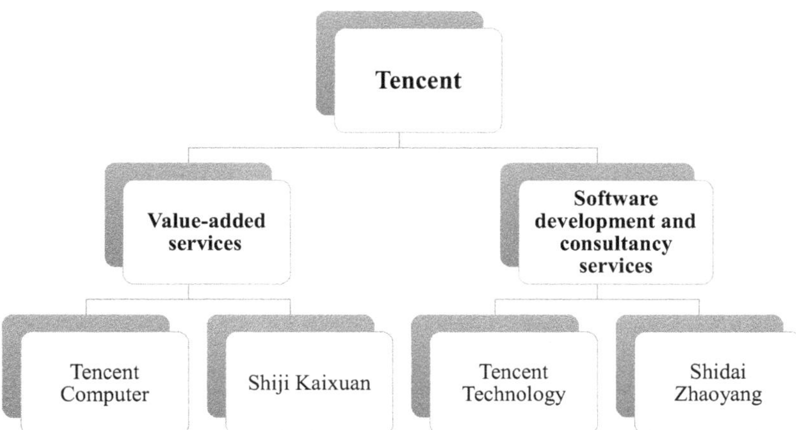

Figure 2.1 Tencent's Structure as of June 2004, Before IPO

Source: Tencent, Prospectus.

for Chinese companies' overseas public listings.[29] In 2004 alone, Goldman Sachs participated in coordinating and underwriting the IPO of Ping An Insurance (Group) Co.—China's second-largest life insurer and third-largest property insurer—on the HKSE, Shanda Interactive Entertainment Limited's IPO on the American NASDAQ, and Tencent's IPO.[30] Tencent's listing in Hong Kong was especially a landmark because it was the first Chinese Internet company "to be listed on the Main Board of the (Hong Kong) Stock Exchange."[31]

Tencent's reports broke down its businesses into three major areas: Internet value-added services (IVAS), mobile and telecommunications value-added services (MVAS), and online advertising. Both IVAS and MVAS were built on the basic IM platform, which allowed users to "communicate via text messages, images, video, voice, and e-mail." These services then created an online community for social networking, entertainment, and gaming. Tencent embedded targeted advertisements into different platforms.[32]

Table 2.2 Tencent's Annual Balance, 2001–18 (RMB Million)

Year	*Total Assets*	*Revenues*	*Net Profit*
2001	66	49	10
2002	214	263	141
2003	576	735	322
2004	2,863	1,144	441
2005	3,427	1,426	485
2006	4,651	2,800	1,064
2007	6,985	3,821	1,568
2008	9,856	7,155	2,816
2009	17,506	12,440	5,222
2010	35,830	19,646	8,115
2011	56,804	28,496	10,225
2012	75,256	43,894	12,785
2013	107,235	60,437	15,563
2014	171,166	78,932	23,888
2015	306,818	102,863	29,108
2016	395,899	151,938	41,447
2017	554,672	237,760	72,471
2018	723,521	312,694	79,984

Sources: Tencent, Annual Reports, 2001–18 (revenue year-end of December 31).[1]

1 For the purpose of accuracy in this table, the RMB is the original data from Tencent's company reports. For the following charts, which aim to show the growth curve of Tencent's businesses, the currency has been changed to USD based on World Bank, "Official Exchange Rate (LCU per US$, Period Average)," accessed March 20, 2017, http://data.worldbank.org/indicator/PA.NUS.FCRF?end=2015&locations=CN&start=1998&view=chart.

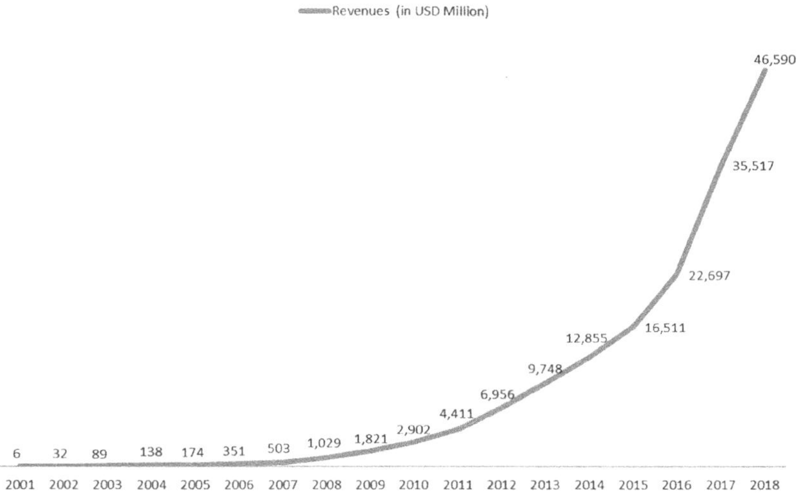

Figure 2.2 Tencent's Annual Revenue Growth, 2001–18

Sources: Tencent, Prospectus and Annual Reports 2004–18 (revenue year-end of December 31).

Table 2.3 Tencent's Revenue by Business, 2001–11

Year	*Revenue*							
	IVAS		*MVAS*		*Online Advertising*		*Other*	
	Total RMB (Millions)	*% of Total*	*Total RMB (Millions)*	*% of Total*	*Total RMB (Millions)*	*% of Total*	*Total RMB (Millions)*	*% of Total*
2001	0.9	1.9	38	77.3	8	15.7	2	4.9
2002	41	15.5	199	75.6	19	7.3	4	1.6
2003	230	31.3	467	63.6	33	4.4	5	0.7
2004	439	38.4	641	56.1	55	4.8	9	0.7
2005	787	55.1	517	36.3	113	7.9	10	0.7
2006	1,825	65.2	700	25.0	267	9.5	8	0.3
2007	2,514	65.8	808	21.1	493	12.9	7	0.2
2008	4,915	68.7	1,399	19.6	826	11.5	15	0.2
2009	9,531	76.6	1,906	15.3	962	7.7	41	0.4
2010	15,482	78.8	2,716	13.8	1,373	7.0	75	0.4
2011	23,043	80.8	3,271	11.5	1,992	7.0	190	0.7

Sources: Tencent, Prospectus, 9; Tencent, Annual Reports, 2004–11 (revenue year-end of December 31).

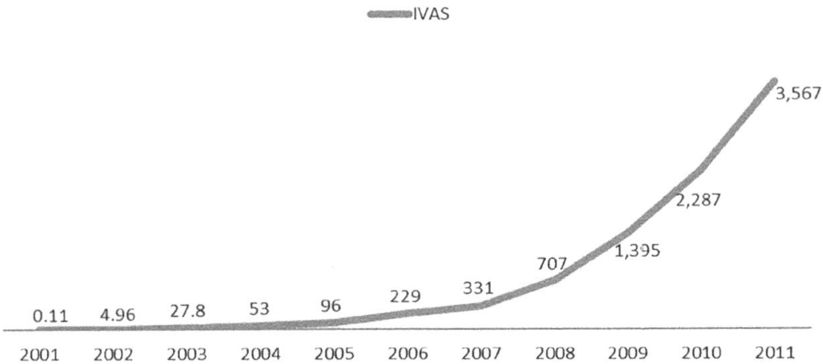

Figure 2.3 Annual Growth in Internet Value-Added Services, 2001–11 (USD in millions)

Sources: Tencent, Prospectus, 9; Tencent, Annual Report, 2004–11 (revenue year-end of December 31).

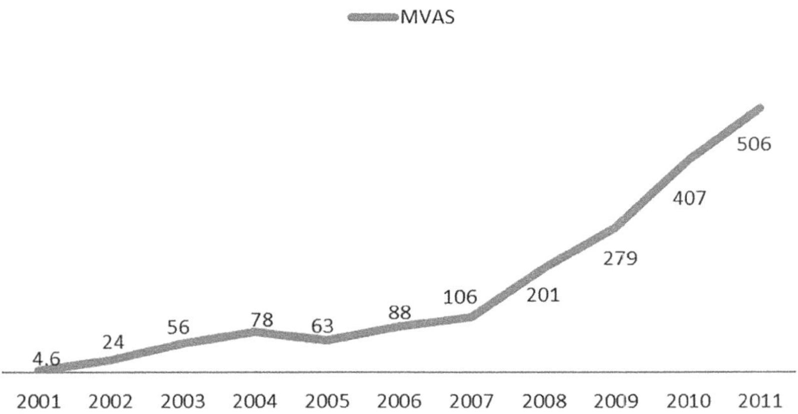

Figure 2.4 Annual Growth in Mobile Value-Added Services, 2001–11 (USD in millions)

Sources: Tencent, Prospectus, 9; Tencent, Annual Report, 2004–11 (revenue year-end of December 31).

With the diffusion of smartphones and the completion of 3G and 4G networks throughout China, MVAS were gradually expanded to games, entertainment, and community networking, parallel to the Internet VAS provided on desktops. Especially after 2011 when Tencent launched Weixin and WeChat, a smartphone-based chatting service, the mobile sector was further strengthened through mobile applications.[33]

In 2012 Tencent reorganized its business structure by "aligning the product development and management" of some core services between PC and mobile versions.[34] Its spreadsheet combined the IVAS and MVAS into one column, value-added services. The spreadsheet also included a new column for revenue from e-commerce transactions. Due to some mergers and acquisitions, discussed later, the revenue of e-commerce was grouped into the "other" column after the first quarter of 2015.[35]

Table 2.4 Tencent's Revenue by Business, 2012–18 (USD in millions)

Year	*Value-Added Services*		*Online Advertising*		*E-Commerce Transactions*		*Other*	
	Amount RMB (Millions)	*% of Total Revenues*	*Amount RMB (Millions)*	*% of Total Revenues*	*Amount RMB (Millions)*	*% of Total Revenues*	*Amount RMB (Millions)*	*% of Total Revenues*
2012	35,718	81	3,382	8	4,428	10	366	1
2013	44,985	75	5,034	8	9,796	16	622	1
2014	63,310	80	8,308	11	4,753	6	2,561	3
2015	80,669	78	17,468	17			4,726	5
2016	107,810	71	26,970	18			17,158	11
2017	153,983	65	40,439	17			43,338	18
2018	176,646	56	58,079	19			77,969	25

Sources: Tencent, Annual Reports, 2012–18 (revenue year-end of December 31).

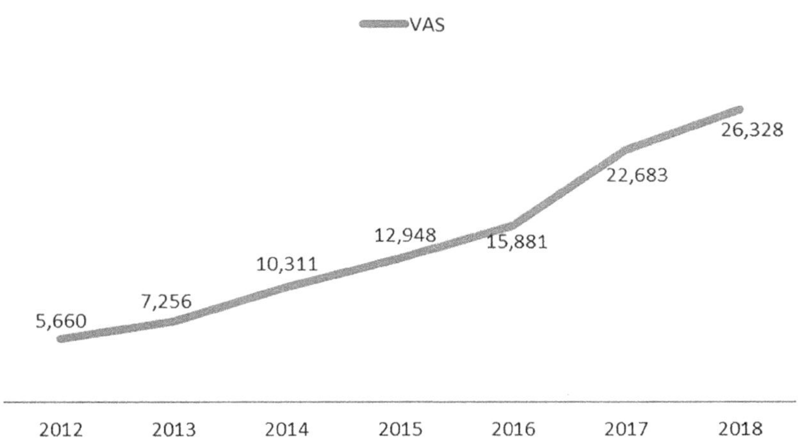

Figure 2.5 Annual Growth in Value-Added Services, 2012–18

Sources: Tencent, Annual Reports, 2012–18 (revenue year-end of December 31).

Dissecting the Tencent Empire

Tencent encompassed a broad range of domestic and international services. A closer look at each major sector of Tencent's businesses, focusing on the company's own product development and processes of diversification, is next in this chapter, with primary attention to the course of Tencent's growth and outreach rather than its inter-capital relations with other Internet companies. Tencent's business evolution exemplifies the processes many political-economy scholars term *commodification* and *diversification*. Mosco defines commodification as the process of transforming a product's use value into exchange value.[36] In this case, it is to monetize the IM service and gain marketable value—be it user traffic or cash flow—from QQ. Diversification, as will be illustrated later, refers to a strategy to diversify product lines out of a company's original business in order to maximize market share and thus profit.

Communications Platforms

Tencent's early success stood primarily on the IM service QQ. Tencent has continuously worked on improving QQ with two important breakthroughs: the launch of business QQ to serve corporate clients for organization communications and the development of Weixin/WeChat on mobile devices in 2011. To avoid redundancy, these most popular products are detailed in Chapter 4 as part of Tencent's cultural profile.

Social Platforms

Tencent also promoted a set of social networks to strengthen its online community: QZone and real-name social-networking site (SNS).

QZone

QZone, launched in 2005 as a featured product in social networking and online community interactions, was a personal home page "bundled with web blog, photo album and online music."[37] Each QQ user automatically received a QZone with his or her QQ numbers. While users posted blogs and photos on QZone, their QQ friends could view and interact with them. Largely drawing traffic from QQ, QZone has quickly become one of the top three social-networking sites (SNS) in China.[38] Another report on global social-network websites put QZone as the third-largest worldwide in 2013, only behind Facebook and YouTube, as it evolved into a major social-networking platform that combined blogging, microblogging, photo sharing, activity posts, and micromarketing promotions.[39] By the end of December 2018, QZone maintained 532.4 million active user accounts via smart devices.[40]

Real-Name Social-Networking Site (SNS)

While QZone is based on QQ accounts using nicknames in the virtual world, Xiaoyou.com, launched in January 2009 by Tencent, is a real-name social-networking site for university students and alumni to make connections.[41] The name of the site was changed to Pengyou.com in 2010, which invites a broader scope of users, including university students and graduates and a wider range of professional communities, such as white-collar workers.[42] At the end of 2012, Pengyou.com reached 247 million active users.[43]

Media Platform

The online portal QQ.com was Tencent's major media portal for news, entertainment, sports, videos, technologies, fashion, automobiles, and shopping, linking to Tencent's VAS.[44] Launched in December 2003, the website served first as an information-distributing center. Tencent launched multiple media campaigns in promoting the QQ.com brand. At the end of 2004, the company put together a one-year anniversary celebration for the website with the slogan, "New life, my style." Targeting young people, Ma Huateng announced at the event that Tencent aimed to make QQ.com the number 1 website for fashion and entertainment in China.[45]

Starting from 2006, QQ.com collaborated with provincial news agencies to build regional news portals as subsites of the main portal.[46] For example, in March 2006 Tencent worked with the *Chongqing Economic Times* to launch cq.qq.com as a local-media portal for Chongqing audiences. The Chinese name of cq.qq.com is Da Yu Wang, which means the website for the area of Yu—the acronym of Chongqing—a southwestern metropolis. Shortly after, Tencent established many more local news portals using the acronyms of different regions. These portals became an important content provider for QQ.com and tightened Tencent's connections to users from different places.

In 2007 Tencent further promoted the QQ.com brand by reporting significant national news and sports events. In 2008 when Sichuan suffered a disastrous earthquake, aside from providing real-time news, QQ.com called for online donations from the audience and ultimately raised more than $3.31 million (RMB 23 million) for the earthquake victims. In 2010 QQ.com worked with the Shanghai World Exposition as the organizer's exclusive Internet service sponsor.[47]

For sports news, the portal leveraged opportunities presented by the 2010 and 2014 World Cups, 2008 and 2012 summer Olympics, and regional events. During the 2008 Beijing Olympics, QQ.com reached a traffic record of 1.1 billion page views a day as it provided comprehensive coverage, including live reports in the form of texts, images, and videos.[48] In 2014 Tencent signed exclusive partnerships with HBO and the National Basketball Association (NBA) to distribute their TV shows and sports events in China, which further enhanced traffic on Tencent's media portal.[49] The sports channel carries a number of subscription packages that provide subscribers with various levels of access to the NBA, the Premier League, the National Collegiate Athletic Association (NCAA), and the National Hockey League (NHL) games.[50] The online streaming portal provides similar services on TV shows and movies, such as early access to newly released movies and the option to skip advertisements when streaming.[51]

Search Engine

In March 2006 Tencent launched its own search engine: Soso.com.[52] Although Baidu dominated China's search-engine market with more than a 70 percent share, Tencent's Soso was the second-leading search engine in China's mobile search market.[53] In September 2013, Tencent made a substantial investment in another search-engine company, Sogou.com, and merged its search-related businesses into Sogou.[54]

Online Advertising

While online advertising has been a foundational profit mechanism in the Internet economy in the U.S., Tencent, unlike the American pioneers of Google, Yahoo, Microsoft, AOL, and Facebook, which "served profile-based targeted advertising and/or collected consumer data across expansive networks," was not able to take full advantage of its tremendous user traffic for advertising revenue until 2007 when it developed targeted online advertising technology.[55] This was partly due to the low diffusion rate of the Internet in China in the early 2000s when "the Internet has not been proven as a widely accepted medium for advertising."[56] According to Tencent's prospectus, revenues from online advertising only accounted for 4.5 percent of its total revenue in 2003.[57] This number grew gradually with the wider diffusion of Internet VAS in China. The large user base of Tencent's IM platforms and VAS, in particular, put the company in an advantageous position, as a 90 percent coverage of Chinese online users made it easy for Tencent to identify their demography, location, preferences, and online context.[58] In March 2011 Tencent further developed a web-based video platform for advertising, which boosted video advertising revenue by 70 percent in the fourth quarter of 2011.[59] The growth of online advertising was entangled with the development of the company's media portal QQ.com, mobile software, and all kinds of VAS.[60]

Online Games

Online gaming stood out as one of the most important contributors to Tencent's VAS. In 2018 the revenue VAS generated was $46.6 billion (RMB 312.69 billion), with $19.14 billion (RMB 128.4 billion) coming from online games.[61] Of the revenue in online games, smartphone games contributed $11.6 billion (RMB 77.8 billion).[62] As another critical element of Tencent's cultural profile, the genres of Tencent's games and expanding strategies are detailed in Chapter 4.

E-Commerce and Online Payment

Business was further extended by an e-commerce sector when Tencent launched a customer-to-customer (C2C) auction platform, Paipai.com, in 2005.[63] The website attracted 230,000 certified sellers with 300,000 commodities for sale within one month of its establishment.[64] Launched together with Paipai.com to assist online transactions was an escrow online payment system, Tenpay.[65] Certified by China Information Security Evaluation Center in 2006, Tenpay was further integrated into Tencent's online system by providing payment services to online phone bills, air flight tickets, and lotteries.[66] To strengthen the e-commerce sector, Tencent launched a new business-to-business-to-consumer (B2B2C) platform, Buy.qq.com, in 2011, which incorporated other institutional e-commerce operators into its platform, such as OkBuy, an online retailer for clothing outfits and shoes; Yixun.com, a website selling digital products and home appliances; and Kela, an online jewelry vendor.[67]

As a latecomer to e-commerce, Tencent faced fierce competition from established players, such as eBay, Alibaba's Taobao, Yipai, and Dangdang.[68] Under such circumstances, in March 2014 Tencent announced a strategic partnership with Jingdong (JD.com)—China's second-largest online retailer.[69] Under the partnership, Tencent transferred all of its e-commerce business into JD.com and embedded JD.com's services into mobile QQ and Weixin/WeChat.[70] This significantly changed both companies' business layouts as well as China's e-commerce industry landscape. Tencent was finally able to compete with Alibaba, while JD advanced its weight in mobile e-commerce. In August 2016 Tencent became JD.com's largest institutional shareholder with 25 percent of its ordinary shares.[71] Details of the deal are elaborated in the section "E-commerce" under "Horizontal Integration."

Research and Development

As an Internet company, Tencent puts a lot of efforts and money in research and development. The expenses in research and development have grown noticeably in recent years.

Tencent established Internet-research academies in Beijing, Shanghai, and Shenzhen in 2007, one year after it announced plans to explore Internet technologies by collaborating with universities in these three cities.[72] Each academy focused on one or more of these six areas: data storage, data mining, multimedia, language processes, distribution network, and wireless technology.[73]

Table 2.5 Research and Development Expenses, 2004–18 (RMB Million)

Year	*R&D*
2004	56
2005	162
2006	297
2007	376
2008	710
2009	1,191
2010	1,685
2011	2,684
2012	4,176
2013	5,095
2014	7,581
2015	9,039
2016	11,845
2017	17,456
2018	22,936

Sources: Tencent, Annual Reports, 2004–18 (revenue year-end of December 31).

In 2008 Tencent established the Tencent Scholarship for Excellence in Science and Technology at top Chinese universities, including Peking University, Tsinghua University, Shanghai Jiaotong University, Huazhong University of Science and Technology, Harbin Institute of Technology, South China University of Technology, Northwestern Polytechnical University, and University of Electronic Science and Technology of China. The company was the first among Chinese Internet enterprises to reward students' talents in computer science.[74] According to the terms with Peking University, for example, every year three students with distinguished academic performance are each awarded $2,173 (RMB 15,000), and another ten students with merits each receive $724 (RMB 5,000).

Labor Practices

Valuing high-tech human resources, Tencent implements attractive employee benefits and bonuses to recruit and reward talented employees. In 2011 the company proposed a three-year Anju Plan to provide no-interest housing loans to employees. Employees who have been with the company for more than three years and need money to buy their first condominium or house could apply to get a loan up to $46,150 (RMB 300,000) from the company; repayments of the loan were deducted from the employee's monthly salary over six years.[75]

Tencent was also very aggressive in its actions against employees leaving for other Internet companies. In November 2008 Tencent filed a legal case against 15 of its former employees who went to 51.com, a leading provider and a competitor with Tencent in social network and game services.[76] According to Tencent, these employees violated their contracts, which stated that they could not join a company in a similar industry within a certain period of time after their departure from Tencent.[77]

In view of the growing competition for talent among high-tech companies, Tencent designed an employee incentive scheme to reward employees with stock shares as bonuses.[78] On July 6, 2016, Tencent issued a total of 56,213,500 new shares to reward 10,383 employees for their loyalty.[79] Based on the closing price of Tencent's shares that day, the market value of the rewards was worth approximately $1.26 billion.[80]

Expansion Through Horizontal and Vertical Integration

Tencent has been actively expanding its businesses through extending control to horizontal and vertical markets, in the form of mergers, acquisitions, and strategic alliances. This section does not aim to exhaustively catalog every single investment Tencent has made but attempts to develop an understanding of Tencent's synergetic empire by scrutinizing the public documents detailing various types of business expansion. Tencent's collaborations with domestic partners experienced several distinct stages. During the early stage between 1998 and 2005, Tencent aimed at growing big and tried to extend its business into as many areas as possible. Starting in 2005, Tencent planned large volumes of acquisitions of and mergers with companies smaller than Tencent to strengthen the businesses it had stakes in. After 2010 Tencent turned to strategic investments and alliances with other strong players in the market, and it acquired minority stakes in those companies—instead of buying the whole company or including the company into its kingdom as a subsidiary. Acquisitions and mergers started as occasional and opportunistic choices but after 2010 became a comprehensive strategy that the Tencent's leadership favored. Altogether, these mergers, acquisitions, and strategic alliances assisted Tencent to horizontally and vertically integrate within the broadly defined Internet VAS.

The analysis is presented primarily by chronicling these stages, and, also organized by tracing Tencent's roadmap into each business market. For simplicity of analysis, "horizontal integration" is defined here as purchasing other companies that operate in the same product markets and at the same level of production, and "vertical integration" as extending control at different levels of production from input through output.[81]

Horizontal Integration

E-mail Service

On March 16, 2005, Tencent acquired a leading Chinese e-mail developer, Foxmail Group, which was Tencent's first formal business acquisition.[82] Foxmail, originally developed by Zhang Xiaolong in 1997, was acquired in 2000 by Boda China, a Guangzhou-based Internet service company, for $1.47 million (RMB 12 million).[83] The Boda China deal moved Zhang and the whole Foxmail research-and-development team to Tencent.[84] Foxmail, occupying the largest share of e-mail service in China, contributed not only 5 million users to Tencent but also its expertise in providing institutional or corporate communication services on a large scale.[85] The deal came at a time when Tencent was in fierce competition with Microsoft's MSN and Hotmail.[86] Zhang, the core founder of Foxmail, also became a leading member of Tencent's research-and-development team and later stood out as the chief architect of Tencent's Weixin/WeChat service.[87]

MVAS

In 2006, Tencent acquired a 100 percent equity interest in two mobile and telecommunications service providers: Joymax Development Ltd. established in 2003 and specializing in providing SMS-based VAS and marketing and branding through mass media, and Wangdian Technology, founded in 2000 in Nanjing and also an MVAS provider.[88]

In 2007 Tencent further strengthened the MVAS sector by acquiring Beijing BIZCOM Technology Co. Ltd. and Beijing Starsinhand Technology Co. Ltd., both of which provide MVAS.[89] On March 20 and May 23, 2008, Tencent acquired 100 percent equity interest in two more domestic mobile and telecommunications VAS providers, Guangzhou Yunxun and Tianjin Shouzhongwanwei, for a total of $1.59 million (RMB 11 million).[90]

Bulletin Board Systems (BBS) and Online Community

In September 2010 Tencent acquired a Beijing-based Internet community software and service provider, the Comsenz Group, as its wholly owned subsidiary for $43 million (RMB 292 million).[91] Comsenz is a leading player in providing online community services, such as social-networking software, bulletin-board systems, and cloud servers in China.[92]

Search Engines

On September 6, 2013, Tencent paid $448 million in cash (RMB 2.741 billion) to Sogou for 36.5 percent of its equity capital.[93] By 2013 Tencent's share in Sogou increased to 40 percent with 24.8 percent of the voting power.[94] Tencent president Lau Chi Ping Martin and chief operating officer Ren Yuxin joined the Sogou board of directors.

Sogou stood as China's third-largest search service provider with a 10 percent share of the market, after Baidu with 63 percent and Qihoo 360 with 18 percent.[95] Sogou owned a line of online and mobile applications, including Sogou Pinyin, a top Chinese-language input software; Sogou browser, a web browser with third-largest market share in China; Sogou Web Directory; mapping; and voice search.[96]

The partnership, coming in a period of a heated competition within China's search-engine market, not only regrouped both companies' related businesses but also helped Tencent keep up in China's Internet industry. At that time, Alibaba and Baidu had just closed a few high-profile acquisitions and investment deals of their own, both marching toward conglomerates. Alibaba, in April 2013, paid $586 million to Sina Weibo for an 18 percent stake in China's leading microblogging service, provoking a head-on confrontation with Tencent's Weixin /WeChat.[97] One month later, Alibaba invested $294 million for 28 percent of shares in an online mapping company, AutoNavi, which in 2014 became a wholly owned subsidiary of Alibaba.[98] Baidu, in July, announced a deal worth $1.9 billion, the largest in China's Internet industry history, to acquire 91 Wireless, China's leading mobile app store operator.[99] All three Internet giants were expanding their territories.

E-commerce

In March 2014 Tencent and JD.com, the second-largest e-commerce operator in China with a 17.5 percent market share, began a strategic collaboration.[100] In the deal Tencent bought 15.0 percent of JD.com for $214.66 million (part of a subscription agreement before JD.com's IPO) and gave JD.com 100 percent interest in the Tencent B2C platform, QQ Wanggou; 100 percent in the C2C site PaiPai; and 9 percent equity interest in Tencent's Yixun.com.[101] Upon JD.com's IPO in May 2014, Tencent further purchased 5 percent shares.[102] On December 2, 2014, Tencent acquired an additional 0.45 percent of JD.com, which gave Tencent overall a 17.88 percent interest in JD.com.[103] Tencent's president Lau was appointed as JD.com's director.[104] Although possessing a large ownership stake, Tencent only held a 3.7 percent voting stake, with JD.com founder Liu Qiangdong maintaining a dominant voting position.[105]

Major considerations of the collaboration were to expand JD.com's mobile market and Tencent's e-commerce business. These were interpreted as a direct countermeasure to the Alibaba–Sina Weibo alliance formed in April 2013 that would create advertising space for Alibaba's Taobao retailers to send customized posts and interact with followers taking advantage of the mass user base on Weibo, the leading microblogging platform.[106]

Vertical Integration

Online Travel Agency: eLong

On May 17, 2011, Tencent formed a strategic partnership with eLong, a China-based, leading online and mobile travel agency listed on NASDAQ, by purchasing about 11 million newly issued shares, which gave Tencent a 16.15 percent equity interest in eLong, at a price of $84.4 million (RMB 548 million).[107] The deal made Tencent the second-largest shareholder of eLong, the first being the U.S.-based online travel giant Expedia with a 56 percent.[108]

As Tencent's first significant investment in the travel market, the collaboration added another piece to Tencent's ever-enlarging online lifestyle kingdom with e-Long's worldwide travel services, such as hotels, flights, resorts, and so on.[109] For eLong and Expedia, Tencent's establishment in Chinese online communities brought users to them.[110] With Xiaoguang Wu, Tencent's senior executive vice president of Internet business, sitting as a member of eLong's board of directors upon the deal, Tencent maintained significant influence in business decisions on eLong.[111]

Online Software Security

Kingsoft Corp. Ltd., a Chinese leading software developer and Internet service provider in Internet security, became a Tencent associate on July 6, 2011, when Tencent acquired a 15.28 percent shareholding in the company for $114 million (HKD 892 million).[112] Tencent president and executive director Lau was appointed as a non-executive director of Kingsoft on July 28, 2011.[113] The alliance came at a time when Tencent was in a cut-throat competition with another Chinese online security firm, Qihoo 360. Bloomberg reported that Kingsoft and Tencent together possessed 20 percent of market share in China's online-security sector, which was only surpassed by Qihoo 360.[114]

In June 2013 Tencent purchased an additional 8 percent of the shares of Kingsoft Internet Security Software Corp. Ltd. (KIS), a non-wholly owned subsidiary of the Kingsoft Group, which was renamed Cheetah Technology Corp. Ltd.,[115] at approximately $47 million (RMB 290 million) and increased its stakes in KIS to 18.0 percent.[116]

Ridesharing and Online Taxi Reservation

In April 2013, Tencent invested $15 million in Didi Dache, a mobile application for taxi reservation or ridesharing and later embedded into the Tencent

Weixin/WeChat system.[117] In January 2014 by further investing in Didi, Tencent aimed to support its competition with Kuaidi Dache, a similar mobile application providing cab-calling services backed by Alibaba.[118] The rivalry between Didi and Kuaidi was so fierce that they both rewarded their customers by reimbursing money to customers, Didi through Tencent's Weixin/WeChat payment and Kuaidi through Alibaba's Alipay.[119] In February 2014 Didi and Kuaidi reached a partnering deal so that they no longer engaged in cutthroat competition with each other.[120]

Logistics and Trade Service

On January 15, 2014, Tencent teamed up with Chinese logistics facilities operator China South City Holdings Ltd., by acquiring 9.9 percent of its shares for $191.6 million (HKD 1.497 billion).[121] Lin Ching Hua (Davis), general manager of Tencent's strategy development department and social and performance advertisement department, was appointed as non-executive director of China South City in June 2014. In September 2014 Tencent further subscribed China South City's shares, raising its interest to 11.55 percent.[122] The strategic partnership connected China South City's offline trade services, warehouse, and logistics expertise to Tencent's online and mobile strengths of e-commerce, marketing, payment solution, and customer reach.[123]

Online Review Platform

In February 2014 Tencent invested in an online review and transaction platform for local businesses—Dianping.com—that offered such services as "local merchant listing, consumer reviews, money saving deals, online reservation and take out ordering."[124] A Yelp.com-like site, Dianping would connect its service to Tencent's mobile ports, including mobile QQ, Weixin, and others. The $500 million deal gave Tencent a 20 percent stake in Dianping and strengthened the network effect through mobile platforms and group buying.[125] For Tencent, this was another step in building a comprehensive ecosystem that advantages its large online user base to provide offline purchasing information and transactions.[126]

In June 2014 Tencent formed an alliance with another online and mobile platform that provided information for location-based local merchants and consumers, 58.com Inc.[127] Tencent invested $736 million (RMB 4.541 billion) in June and $140 million (RMB 863 million) in September in exchange for a total 24.0 percent stake.[128] Tencent's Wu became a member of 58.com's board of directors in August 2014.[129] In 2015, after some reorganization, Tencent held 22.9 percent of 58.com's equity interest.[130] The partnership added one more piece to Tencent's online-to-offline services, with 58.com's specialty in serving local merchants and consumers for classified business information.

Online Real-Estate Service

In March 2014 Tencent made a $180 million (RMB 1.102 billion) investment in Leju Holdings Ltd., a Chinese online-to-offline real-estate services provider, and Tencent's president Lau was appointed a director in Leju.[131] Before the trade, Leju was a wholly owned subsidiary of E-House, a Chinese real-estate company, listed on the New York Stock Exchange since 2007 with services of e-commerce, online advertising, brokerage and marketing, real-estate databases, financing, and community-based VAS.[132] On April 22, 2014, Leju was publicly listed on the New York Stock Exchange, and Tencent put in an additional $20 million (RMB 125 million) for Leju's shares to maintain a 15 percent stake.[133] The alliance primarily targeted the mobile-based, real-estate e-commerce market by bringing Leju's online real-estate service to Tencent's mobile platforms, promoting Leju's brand through Weixin/WeChat official accounts and providing mobile payment access to Leju's users.[134]

Digital Mapping

In April 2014, Tencent became the second major stakeholder in NavInfo Co. Ltd. by subscribing approximately 11.28 percent of the company's share capital of $187.6 million (RMB 1.173 billion).[135] The NavInfo, China-based and listed on the Shenzhen Stock Exchange, provided geographical information services, such as digital mapping, telematics, instant traffic updates, and location-based big-data applications.[136] Owning nine wholly owned companies, 11 holding companies, and six joint-stock companies, the company claimed to be China's largest and the world's third-largest digital map provider, supplying a number of automakers' in-dash navigation systems in China, including BMW, Volkswagen, Mercedes-Benz, General Motors, Volvo, Ford, SAIC Motor, Toyota, Nissan, Hyundai, Peugeot, and Citroen.[137]

Although Tencent has displayed distinctive expanding strategies by horizontal and vertical integration, some caveats need to be pointed out in these processes. Due to the widely spread scope and categories of online VAS, there are lacks of clear boundaries between different strategies. Different services often coexist within one application, where forms of expansion are also entangled. Tencent's business expansions, for example, have combined horizontal integration, vertical integration, and a more general process of diversification. The company first expanded into many business areas by diversifying its own business scopes, as discussed in a prior section. Then, Tencent horizontally expanded in some service markets in which it already had a strong presence, such as e-mail, IM, online community and BBS, media portal, search engine, and e-commerce. In other areas that provided online-to-offline connections and tied new apps to Tencent's messaging and communication portals, the company expanded through the form of vertical integration. With the reach and scale of the businesses becoming so broad now, one particular business move, very often, could entail a number of different strategies. This has actually become a salient feature of the Internet industry, that the breadth and depth of the services very often intersect, and therefore some boundaries get blurred.

Diversification Under Internet Plus

In addition to horizontal and vertical integration, under China's recent national policy of Internet Plus, which was to build a social economic network around an integrated online to offline platform through the Internet, Tencent also started a more encompassing diversifying strategy around 2013, on a scale much broader and deeper than previous ones.

Investment Advisory

In November 2014 Tencent acquired a 23 percent stake in CITIC Capital Holdings Ltd., an investment management and advisory company with strong ties to the Chinese state, for $263 million (HKD 2.040 billion).[138] The deal, under a round of the CITIC Group's additional share offering, was expected to boost collaboration on Internet finance between the two companies.[139] Relying on CITIC's expertise in investment and finance, Tencent would also enhance its own investment profile. In 2015 alone the two together participated in at least three major investments in Chinese technology companies.[140] In 2016 CITIC Capital joined Tencent's consortium to buy the Finnish game developer Supercell as a co-investor.[141]

Banking

On December 16, 2014, Tencent, together with other partners including Shenzhen Baiyeyuan Investment Co. Ltd. and Shenzhen Li Ye Group Co. Ltd., were granted a license by the state's banking regulatory commission to establish a privately owned commercial bank, Shenzhen WeBank Ltd., in which Tencent held 30 percent interest.[142] In January 2015 WeBank started to provide loans to small- and medium-size businesses. The move came under China's government's relaxation in banking and financial systems, which allowed privately owned lenders to operate banks under a pilot program.[143] Tencent was one of the few approved companies to establish private banks, as was Alibaba.[144]

Media and the Film Industry

Tencent had been preparing for years to set foot in the media and film industries. In May 2011 Tencent made an initial step into the movie industry by buying a 4.60 percent stake in Huayi Brothers Media Corp., a Chinese giant in film production and publicly listed on the Shenzhen Stock Exchange since

2009.[145] With an investment of $69 million (RMB 445 million), Tencent became the largest institutional shareholder in China's biggest nonstate film company.[146] The deal was made at a premium of 9.89 percent over Huayi Brothers' regular stock price, indicating Tencent's eagerness for entering the market.[147] Tencent and Huayi Brothers started their strategic partnership in December 2011 in movie production, content distribution, and online promotion. At the time of Tencent's investment, the two primary individual shareholders were Wang Zhongjun and Wang Zhonglei, the cofounders of the company, who held 26.14 percent and 8.27 percent stakes, respectively. Meanwhile, Jack Ma, Alibaba Group's founder and chairman, became an investor in Huayi Brothers in 2006 and sat on the board of directors of the film company as the third-largest shareholder with 5.50 percent shares.[148]

In the same year, Tencent put another $17.14 million (HKD 132 million), for 5.01 percent stake in the Hong Kong-based film production and distribution company Media Asia Group Holdings Ltd.[149]

Tencent continued exploring the movie industry in 2012 when it acquired 619,400,000 ordinary shares of ChinaVision Media Group Ltd.[150] The deal, worth $31.713 million (HKD 247.76 million), gave Tencent an 8 percent stake in the HKEX-listed and mainland-based television and cinema content producer and distributor.[151] Similar to Tencent's Huayi Brother investments, the ChinaVision deal was made at a premium of 8.7 percent to its closing price.[152] However, in March 2014, Alibaba Group bought a 60 percent stake and became the controlling shareholder of ChinaVision, which was renamed Alibaba Pictures Group Ltd. in August 2014.[153]

In 2015 Tencent established its own movie production unit, Penguin Pictures.[154] So far the company has participated in the production and distribution of several Hollywood big-screen movies, such as *Warcraft*, *Kong: Skull Island*, *Wonder Woman*, *Venom*, *Bumblebee*, and *Terminator 6*, among others.[155]

Conclusion

Tencent's pattern of business expansion featured a combination of horizontal and vertical integration and a widening diversification. Not many documents indicate the financial sources of these investments. Limited texts from Tencent's own financial reports and trade journals suggest a majority of these investments were self-funded, while several other deals were done through fund-raising from bank loans and investment partners.[156]

Tencent's collaboration with other domestic Internet companies or technology investors demonstrates a strategic choice of acquisitions, mergers, and partnerships. If it is acknowledged that Tencent achieved half of its horizontal integration by its own business exploration, then the other half was strengthened through acquisitions and mergers. For example, in areas of its strength, such as online and mobile VAS and QQ- and mobile QQ-related online-community communication, Tencent mostly took a horizontal-integration approach by acquiring smaller companies in the same area.

Vertical integration was accomplished to different extents where Tencent formed strong alliances with other leading players in various businesses. Especially after 2010, Tencent started massively investing in many segments: online traveling, e-commerce, media and film production, online publishing, search engine, online real estate, digital mapping, online taxi calling and ridesharing, online local life service, online entertainment (video and music streaming), and online banking. While most of these expansions were built around its mobile communication platform Weixin/WeChat, Tencent achieved a comprehensive and seamlessly connected online-offline living complex. In its deals with eLong, Sogou, and JD.com, for instance, is a typical model of vertical integration through the exhibition and distribution of offline services on Tencent's online platforms.

Diversification has become a priority, shown not only in Tencent's full-scale investments in the various Internet services but also in its most recent collaborations with investment, finance, and banking businesses. This is not only about Tencent's collaboration with other banking or financial institutions to provide their services via Tencent's platforms; it is more of a sign of Tencent's ambition to become a major player in investment and financial service provision. Such an ambition not only corresponds to the trend to diversify one's business in a media industry but also reflects the special context in China, where the overall political economy now is expected to restructure around the central pivot of the Internet—a national strategy referred by the Chinese state as Internet Plus. Under such context, Tencent no longer binds itself to the businesses that are only online in the traditional senses and starts building a complex of one-stop style in online-offline living and incorporating all the living necessities for individuals. For the moment, a large portion of this plan is synergized entirely on the single mobile application, Weixin/WeChat, which, in turn, reinforces a network effect and reconsolidates Tencent's ability in capturing users.[157]

Tencent's pattern of expansion through horizontal and vertical integration and diversification is parallel to those of U.S. Internet giants.[158] Though initially and still disproportionately bred in China, the outline of Tencent's growing businesses is similar to those of Google, Facebook, and Amazon.

Last but not least, a roadmap of Tencent's growth also indicates the dynamic inter-capital relations in China's Internet industry.[159] The company's achievement largely depends on its successful alliances with a number of leading Internet companies in China. These collaborations also have to be understood under the dynamics of fierce rivalries within China's Internet industry as responses to competitors. The inter-capital collaboration and rivalry, always going hand-in-hand, must be analyzed as two sides of the capital and power reproduction process.

Notes

1. Bloomberg, "TCEHY Stock Quote," January 11, 2019, accessed www.bloomberg.com/quote/TCEHY:US; Tencent, "Tencent Announces Strategic Upgrade," press release, October 1, 2018; "About Tencent"; Tencent, Annual Report, 2015, 5–6.
2. Haibo Zou, "Tengxun shichang celue fenxi" 腾讯市场策略分析 [An Analysis of Tencent's Market Strategy], *Modern Information* 5 (2005): 201–6.
3. Junjie Zhang, "Zhongguo Hulianwang qiye fazhan moshi tanxi—yi Tengxun weili" 中国互联网企业发展模式探析—以腾讯为例 [Exploring Chinese Internet Companies' Developing Model—A Case Study on Tencent], *Economy and Management* 2 (2011): 43–46.
4. Haoqi Dang, "Cong chuanboxue jiaodu jiegou weixin de xinxi chuanbo moshi" 从传播学角度解构微信的信息传播模式 [A Communication Approach to Understand the Model of Wexin], *Southeast Communication* 7 (2012): 71–78.
5. Shijie Wang, "Guanyu Weixin yingxiao xianzhuang ji duice de sikao" 关于微信营销现状及对策的思考 [Some Thoughts on the Status and Strategies of Weixin Marketing], *China Computer and Communication* 1 (2014): 111–13.
6. Annie Liao, Clyde Eirikur Hull, and Rajendran Sriramachandramurthy, "The Six Facets Model of Technology Management: A Study in the Digital Business Industry," *International Journal of Innovation and Technology Management* 10, no. 4 (2013): 1–24; Edward Tse, "Competing on the Edge: Chinese Conglomerates and Changes in Business Strategy," *China Business Review*, July 2015, 1.
7. Tencent, Prospectus, 21, 192.
8. Latzko Toth, "Metaphors of Synchrony: Emergence and Differentiation of Online Chat Devices," *Bulletin of Science, Technology, and Society* 30, no. 5 (2010): 362–74.
9. Jaredet Sandberg, "Net Gain," *Newsweek*, December 7, 1998, 46.
10. Qiu, *Working-Class Network Society*, 22–23.
11. Tencent, Prospectus, 87.
12. "Tencent History," *Tencent*, n.d., accessed August 16, 2016, www.tencent.com/zh-cn/at/rm/2003.shtml.
13. Ibid., 192.
14. Di Wu, "Zhongguo Hulianwang gongsi fenfen lian zhuce Kaiman Qundao" 中国互联网公司纷纷离岸注册开曼群岛 [Chinese Internet Companies Registered in Offshore Cayman Islands], *Zhongguo Xinwen Wang* 中国新闻网, May 16, 2011, accessed November 25, 2016, http://tech.sina.com.cn/i/2011-05-16/10095529207.shtml.
15. Tencent, Prospectus, 21, 192.
16. "Tencent History."
17. Ping Ning, "OICQ xue Disini yaoguo sandao kan" QICQ 学迪斯尼要过三道坎 [OICQ Has to Overcome Three Difficulties Like Disney], *China Business Journal*, April 17, 2001, 2.
18. Zhang Zhao, "Long Conflict Over QQ Continues into Court," *China Daily Asia*, July 24, 2013, accessed August 16, 2016, www.chinadailyasia.com/special/2013-07/24/content_15079749.html.
19. Wang Xing, "A Mysterious Message Millionaire," *China Daily*, January 12, 2009, accessed August 16, 2016, www.chinadaily.com.cn/business/2009-01/12/content_7388202.htm; Yizhen Zhang, "Tengxun xinban OICQ gengming he bianlian de qishi" 腾讯新版OICQ 更名"和"变脸"的启示 [Thoughts from Tencent's Newly Launched Version of OICQ], *eNews*, April 10, 2001, accessed August 16, 2016, http://text.news.sohu.com/11/52/news144665211.shtml.

20. "Internet Timeline of China 1986~2003."
21. "Shanxi Yidong Shenzhen Tengxun lianshou kaitong yidong QQ" 陕西移动深圳腾讯练手开通移动QQ [Shanxi Mobile and Shenzhen Tencent Worked Together to Launch Mobile QQ], *Renmin Youdian* 人民邮电, August 31, 2001, 5.
22. Tencent, Prospectus, 72–73.
23. Ibid., 6.
24. Ibid., 72–73.
25. "National Enterprise Credit Information System," accessed August 16, 2016, www.szcredit.com.cn/web/GSZJGSPT/QyxyDetail.aspx?rid=4f02a8c497e9410d947a29978e6f91b7.
26. "Financial Release of 2004," *Tencent*, June 16, 2004, accessed November 29, 2016, www.tencent.com/en-us/news_timeline.html.
27. Working Group on Ten Years of Tencent, *"Tengxun shi nian"* 腾讯十年 *[Ten Years of Tencent]* (深圳报业集团出版社, 2011), chap. 40, "Shangshi zhi lu" 上市之路 [Road to IPO], n.d., accessed November 29, 2016, http://quanben-xiaoshuo.com/read/21/tengxunshinian/1/40.html.
28. Ibid.
29. Erin P. Flanagin, Alex Fogel, George H. Hines, and Jason M. Kephart, "Goldman Sachs: Strategy for Success," accessed November 29, 2016, www.mcafee.cc/Classes/BEM106/Papers/2006/GS.pdf.
30. Yaohua Chen, Lijun Sheng, and Di Pan, *"Jinrong qiye rongtouzi celue yu caozuo"* 金融企业融投资策略与操作 *[Financial Companies' Strategies and Operations for Investment]* (Beijing: China Industry and Commerce, 2005), 96.
31. Dario De Wet, "Tencent Holdings Limited: An IPO Case Study" (Master's thesis, Department of Finance and Tax, University of Cape Town, 2015), 4, no. 29, accessed November 29, 2016, https://open.uct.ac.za.
32. Tencent, Prospectus, 5, 82, 92.
33. Tencent, Annual Report, 2012, 6.
34. Ibid., 8.
35. Ibid., 12.
36. Mosco, *The Political Economy of Communication*, 129–36.
37. Ibid., 12.
38. Kai Lukoff, "China's Top Four Social Networks: RenRen, Kaixin001, Qzone, and 51.com," *VentureBeat*, April 7, 2010, accessed December 14, 2016, http://venturebeat.com/2010/04/07/chinas-top-4-social-networks-renren-kaixin001-qzone-and-51-com/.
39. "Top 24 Social Networks Worldwide: Facebook, YouTube, and Qzone Lead the Way," *Digital Strategy Consulting*, October 31, 2013, accessed December 14, 2016, www.digitalstrategyconsulting.com/intelligence/2013/10/top_24_social_networks_worldwide_facebook_youtube_and_qzone_lead_the_way.php#more.
40. Tencent, "Tencent Announces 2018 Fourth Quarter and Annual Results," 6.
41. Ibid., 7.
42. Ibid., 10.
43. This was the latest official account of Pengyou.com usage by Tencent.
44. Tencent, Prospectus, 8.
45. Jian Li, "Tengxun tui qingnian menhu zhanlue qiangwei yule neirong shichang" 腾讯推青年门户战略抢位娱乐内容市场 [Tencent Launched Youth Portal Strategy in Order to Compete in Entertainment Content Market], *Tongxin xinxi bao*通信信息报, December 22, 2004, B5.
46. Zhen Liu, "Tengxun quandi quyu menhu" 腾讯圈地区域门户 [Tencent Marched into Regional Media Portal (market)], *21st Century Business Herald*, July 5, 2006, 19.

47. Tencent, Annual Report, 2007, 9; 2008, 7.
48. Ibid., 7.
49. Ibid., 9.
50. "Sports Membership," *Tencent*, accessed December 14, 2016, http://vip.sports.qq.com/.
51. "Video Membership," *Tencent*, accessed December 14, 2016, http://kf.qq.com/faq/120312BfIry6160812qmUzeI.html.
52. Xian Sheng, "Tengxun sousuo: Dong jing zhijian de zhanlue xin jueze" 腾讯搜索：动静之间的战略新抉择 [Tencent's Search Business: A New Strategic Choice], *Jingli Ribao* 经理日报, July 27, 2007, C2.
53. Tencent, Annual Report, 2011, 7.
54. Ibid., 7.
55. Matthew Crain, "Financial Markets and Online Advertising: Reevaluating the Dotcom Investment Bubble," *Information, Communication, and Society* 17, no. 3 (2014): 371–84; Matthew Crain, "Revolution Will Be Commercialized: Finance, Public Policy, and the Construction of Internet Advertising" (Ph.D. diss., Communications, University of Illinois, Urbana-Champaign, 2013), 251.
56. Tencent, Prospectus, 11.
57. Ibid., 6.
58. Jin Sun, "Shangxian guanggao jingzhun dingxiang xitong Tengxun yu rang butong yonghu kandao butong guanggao" 上线广告精准定向系统腾讯欲让不同用户看到 不同广告" [Tencent Aiming at Customizing Online Advertising], *China Business News* 第一财经日报, December 7, 2007, C4.
59. Tencent, Annual Report, 2011, 10.
60. Ibid., 9.
61. Tencent, "Tencent Announces 2018 Fourth Quarter and Annual Results."
62. Ibid.
63. Lei Zhao, "Tengxun chuji C2C" 腾讯出击C2C [Tencent Entered C2C], *Zhonghua Gongshang Shibao IT Tongxun Zhoukan* 中华工商时报*IT*通讯周刊, September 14, 2005, 13.
64. Jun Jiang, "Sanjia mache ladong Tengxun pingtai shengji" 三驾马车拉动腾讯平台升级 [Three Driving Forces Upgraded Tencent's Platform], *Minying Jingji Bao*民营经济报, October 18, 2005, C2.
65. Tencent, Annual Report, 2005, 5.
66. Shan Jiang, "Tengxun caifutong tuijin Zhongguo dianzi zhifu guifanhua" 腾讯财付通推进中国电子支付规范化 [Tencent's Tenpay Facilitated E-Payment Standardization in China], *Zhonghua Gongshang Shibao*中华工商时报, December 27, 2006, 10; Jinping Huang, "Tengxun: Quanmin gongdi de xin qianbao" 腾讯：全民公敌的新钱包 [Tencent's New Money Pocket], *Southern Weekly*南方周末, August 5, 2010, D17.
67. Tencent, Annual Report, 2011, 7; "Tengxun chaoji dianzi shangwu pingtai buy.qq.com" 腾讯超级电子商务平台buy.qq.com [Tencent Launched Super E-Commerce Platform Buy qq.com], *Keji Tai* 科技台, September 20, 2011, www.kejitai.com/shishenme-157-1.html.
68. Yup Lu, "Tengxun muqian bu zhiwang Paipai yingli" 腾讯目前不指望拍拍盈利 [Tencent Is Not Expecting Paipai.com to Profit at the Moment], *China Business News* 第一财经日报, March 14, 2006, C4.
69. Paul Carsten, "Tencent-JD.com Partnership Goes Straight for Alibaba's Throat," *Reuters*, March 10, 2014, accessed August 20, 2016, www.reuters.com/article/jd-tencent-hldg-idUSL3N0M70JY20140310.
70. Tencent, Annual Report, 2013, 9.

71. Qionghui Wang, "Tengcun cheng Jingdong diyi da gudong xutui yidong shejiao dianshang zhanlue" 腾讯成京东第一大股东 续推移动社交电商战略 [Tencent Became Jingdong's no. 1 Stakeholder to Further Promote Mobile E-Commerce], *Caixin Wang* 财新网, August 19, 2016, accessed August 20, 2016, http://companies.caixin.com/2016-08-20/100979849.html.
72. Quanfeng Zhu, "Tengxun chengli yanjiuyuan zhugong liuda hexin jishu" 腾讯成立研究院 主攻六大核心技术 [Tencent Launched Research Institute Aiming at Six Core Technologies], *Jisuanji Shijie* 计算机世界, October 22, 2007, A07; Mo Zhang, "Tengxun touzi yiyuan choujian Hulianwang yanjiuyuan" 腾讯投资亿元筹建互联网研究院 [Tencent Cast Hundreds of Millions to Establish Research Academies], *Zhongguo Gaoxin jinshu chanye daobao* 中国高新技术产业导报, October 30, 2006, B08.
73. Zhu, "Tengxun chengli yanjiuyuan zhugong liuda hexin jishu", A07.
74. "Tengxun zai quanguo zhongdian gaoxiao shou she zhuoyue jiangxuejin" 腾讯在全国重点高校首设卓越奖学金 [Tencent Launched Scholarships for Academic Excellence in Top Chinese Universities], *Keji Ribao* 科技日报, July 1, 2008, 6.
75. Jingke Zhang, "Tengxun gongbu Anju jihua xize gei yuangong zuigao 30 wan mianxi daikuan" 腾讯公布安居计划细则给员工最高30万免息贷款 [Tencent Announced Details of "Anju Plan"], *China Business News* 第一财经日报, June 28, 2011, B03.
76. Liming Zhang and Lihua Gao, "Tengxun wajiao shijian wu yingjia geren yao kaolv xinyong daijia" 腾讯挖角事件无赢家 个人要考虑信用代价 [No Winner in the Incident of Undermining Tencent's Human Resources], *Jingli Ribao* 经理日报, November 24, 2008, A03; "Company Overview," *51.com*, accessed August 20, 2016, www.51.com/company/en.
77. Ibid.
78. Tencent, Annual Report, 2013, 164.
79. "Issue of New Shares Pursuant to Share Award Scheme," *HKEX News*, July 6, 2016, accessed December 14, 2016, www.hkexnews.hk/listedco/listconews/SEHK/2016/0706/LTN201607061191.pdf.
80. Ibid.; "US Dollar (USD) to Hong Kong Dollar (HKD) Exchange Rate History," n.d., accessed December 14, 2016, www.exchangerates.org.uk/USD-HKD-exchange-rate-history.html.
81. Murdock and Golding, "For a Political Economy."
82. Tencent, Annual Report, 2005, 114.
83. "Official Exchange Rate (LCU per US$), Period Average," *World Bank*, 2017, accessed August 29, 2016, http://data.worldbank.org; "Foxmail bianxie zhe Zhang Xiaolong chengwei Boda Gongsi fu zongcai" Foxmail编写者张小龙成为博大公司副总裁 [The Programmer of Foxmail Became Vice President of Boda], *Sina Tech*, April 18, 2000, accessed August 29, 2016, http://tech.sina.com.cn/news/it/2000-04-18/23063.shtml.
84. Weixing Lu, "Tengxun 500 wan meiyuan shougou Foxmail xiayibu yu Wangyi hebing?" 腾讯500万美元收购Foxmail 下一步与网易合并? [Tencent Bought Foxmail for $5 Million], *Shanghai Qingnian Bao*, March 18, 2005, accessed August 29, 2016, http://biz.163.com/05/0318/14/1F4PLUBA00020QBS.html.
85. Yijian Zhang, "Tengxun weishenme yao shougou Foxmail" 腾讯为什么要收购Foxmail [Why Did Tencent Buy Foxmail], *Sina Tech*, April 8, 2005, accessed August 29, 2016, http://tech.sina.com.cn/i/2005-04-08/1746576584.shtml.
86. Ibid.

87. Tencent, "Management Team," *Tencent*, accessed March 6, 2017, www.tencent.com/en-us/company.html.
88. "Tencent to Acquire Wireless Service Provider," *Tencent*, accessed August 29, 2016, www.tencent.com/en-us/content/ir/news/2006/attachments/20060116.pdf; "Tengxun jiang shougou wuxian zengzhi fuwu tigong shang Zhuoyimaisi" 腾讯将收购无线增值服务提供商卓意麦斯 [Tencent About to Acquire Wireless Value-Added Service Provider Joymax], *Sina Tech*, January 16, 2006, accessed August 29, 2016, http://tech.sina.com.cn/i/2006-01-16/1810821683.shtml; Tencent, Annual Report, 2006, 118.
89. Ibid., 120.
90. Ibid., 168.
91. Tencent, Annual Report, 2010, 183.
92. "Introduction to Comsenz," *Sequoia Capital*, accessed February 13, 2017, www.sequoiacap.com/china/en/companies/comsenz/; Comsenz Company Profile, www.bloomberg.com/profiles/companies/COMSENZ:CH-comsenz-inc.
93. "Financial Releases of 2013: Sohu, Sogou, and Tencent Jointly Announce Strategic Cooperation," *Tencent*, accessed August 31, 2016, www.tencent.com/en-us/news_timeline.html.
94. Tencent, Annual Report, 2013, 143.
95. Eric Pfanner, "Web Giant in China Invests in Search Site," *International Herald Tribune*, September 18, 2013, 20.
96. "Financial Releases of 2013."
97. Pfanner, "Web Giant in China."
98. Sarah Rabil and Brian Womack, "Alibaba Agrees to Buy AutoNavi in $1.5 Billion Map Deal," *Bloomberg*, April 11, 2014, accessed August 31, 2016, www.bloomberg.com/news/articles/2014-04-11/alibaba-agrees-to-buy-autonavi-in-1-5-billion-mapping-deal.
99. Lulu Yilun Chen, "Baidu Pays $1.9 Billion in Biggest Takeover to Gain Mobile Share," *Bloomberg*, July 16, 2013, accessed August 31, 2016, www.bloomberg.com/news/articles/2013-07-16/baidu-to-buy-91-wireless-for-1-9-billion-to-add-app-store.
100. Sophie Yu, "Tencent in Bid to Boost W-Commerce Presence," *South China Morning Post*, January 16, 2014, 4.
101. Tencent, Annual Report, 2013, 188; Bien Perez and Sophie Yu, "Tencent's JD Deal Puts the Heat on Alibaba," *South China Morning Post*, March 11, 2014, 3.
102. "Financial Releases of 2014: JD.com and Tencent Form Strategic Partnership to Transform eCommerce Industry in China," *Tencent*, accessed September 2, 2016, www.tencent.com/en-us/news_timeline.html.
103. Tencent, Annual Report, 2014, 142.
104. JD.com, Annual Report, 2014, 123.
105. Chris Nolter, "JD.com Shares Rise in Debut," *The Deal Pipeline*, May 22, 2014.
106. Lize Zhang, "Survival and Development of Chinese New Media Business: Among State, Market, and Public" (Master's thesis, National University of Singapore, Singapore, 2016); Tracey Xiang, "Sina Weibo Monetization Finally Takes Off," *China Daily*, September 4, 2013, accessed September 2, 2016, www.chinadaily.com.cn/business/tech/2013-09/04/content_16942500.htm.
107. Tencent, Annual Report, 2011, 139; Bien Perez, "Tencent Buys Stake in Travel Agency eLong," *South China Morning Post*, May 18, 2011.
108. Perez, "Tencent Buys Stake."
109. "Financial Release of 2011: Tencent Acquires 16% of eLong in Strategic Investment, Expedia, Inc. Co-invests," *Tencent*, May 17, 2011, accessed August 30, 2016, www.tencent.com/en-us/news_timeline.html.

110. Perez, "Tencent Buys Stake."
111. "Board of Directors," *eLong*, May 21, 2013, accessed August 16, 2016, www.elong.net/aboutus/backup_20130521/board_directors.html.
112. "Financial Release of 2011: Tencent Acquires 15.68% of Kingsoft in Strategic Investment," *Tencent*, accessed August 30, 2016, www.tencent.com/en-us/news_timeline.html; Tencent, Annual Report, 2011, 139.
113. "Board of Directors," *Kingsoft*, accessed August 30, 2016, http://ir.kingsoft.com/phoenix.zhtml?c=189890&p=irol-govBoard.
114. Mark Lee, "Tencent Buys $115 Million Kingsoft Stake to Expand Security," *Bloomberg*, July 7, 2011, accessed August 30, 2016, www.bloomberg.com/news/articles/2011-07-06/tencent-agrees-to-buy-15-7-stake-in-kingsoft-for-115-million.
115. "Connected Transaction Issue of Series B Preferred Shares by KIS to the Company and TCH," 2013 Announcements, *Kingsoft*, June 23, 2007, accessed August 31, 2016, http://ir.kingsoft.com/phoenix.zhtml?c=189890&p=irol-Announcements&nyo=3.
116. Tencent, Annual Report, 2013, 143.
117. Zheng Wu and Vanessa Plao, "China Ride App Raises $700 Million," *International New York Times*, December 12, 2014, 21; Xiuqian Zong, "Touziren jiangshu didi kuaidi hebing beihou de gushi" 投资人讲述滴滴快的合并背后的故事 [The Story Behind Didi and Kuaidi's Merge], *Tech.qq.com* 腾讯科技, accessed September 2, 2016, http://tech.qq.com/a/20150304/011410.htm.
118. Wu and Plao, "China Ride App."
119. "China's Mobile Payment War Escalates," *China Daily*, February 22, 2014.
120. Feng Liao, "Didi Kuaidi lianyin" 滴滴快的"联姻：仅22天完成合并计划补贴或降 [Didi and Kuaidi Started Collaborating], *Jinghua Shibao* 京华时报, February 15, 2015, accessed September 2, 2016, http://news.xinhuanet.com/fortune/2015-02/15/c_1114373031.htm.
121. Tencent, Annual Report, 2014, 143.
122. South China City, Annual Report, 2014–15, 25, accessed August 31, 2016, www.chinasouthcity.com/en/ir/.
123. "Financial Releases of 2014: Tencent Makes Strategic Investment in China South City," *Tencent*, January 15, 2014, accessed August 31, 2016, www.tencent.com/en-us/news_timeline.html.
124. "Financial Releases of 2014: Dianping and Tencent Jointly Announce Strategic Cooperation," *Tencent*, accessed September 2, 2016, www.tencent.com/en-us/news_timeline.html.
125. Ibid.
126. Lina Choi and Gary Lau, "Tencent's Investment in Dianping Is Credit Positive," *Moody's Investors Service*, February 20, 2014, accessed September 2, 2016, www.moodys.com/research/MoodysTencents-investment-in-Dianping-is-credit-positive-PR_293296.
127. Tencent, Annual Report, 2014, 143.
128. Ibid.
129. 58.com, Annual Report, 2014, 85, accessed August 31, 2016, http://58.investorroom.com/index.php?s=120.
130. Ibid., 141.
131. "Board of Directors," *Leju.com*, accessed August 31, 2016, http://ir.leju.com/phoenix.zhtml?c=252998&p=irol-govboard; "Financial Releases of 2014: E-House and Tencent Announce Tencent's Strategic Investment in Leju," *Tencent*, March 21, 2014, accessed August 31, 2016, www.tencent.com/en-us/news_timeline.html.

132. "Company Overview," *E-House China*, accessed August 31, 2016, www.ehousechina.com/1defining.htm.
133. Tencent, Annual Report, 2014, 142.
134. "Financial Releases of 2014: E-House and Tencent Announce."
135. Tencent, Annual Report, 2014, 143; "SASAC Approves China Survey's Navinfo Stake Transfer to Tencent," *China Business News*, May 22, 2014.
136. "About Us," *NavInfo*, accessed August 31, 2016, www.navinfo.com/en/aboutus/index.aspx.
137. Ibid.
138. Tencent, Annual Report, 2014, 144; Jonathan Browning, "Citic Adds Investors Including Tencent, Och-Ziff to Share Sale," *Bloomberg*, June 17, 2014, accessed February 16, 2017, www.bloomberg.com/news/articles/2014-06-17/citic-adds-investors-including-tencent-och-ziff-to-share-sale.
139. Jiadai Jiang, "Tengxun rugu Xinzhongxin" 腾讯入股"新中信" 第二批机构投资者另类出场 [Tencent Invested in CITIC Capital Holdings], *21st Century Business Herald 21*世纪经济报道, June 18, 2014, accessed February 16, 2017, http://it.sohu.com/20140618/n400984094.shtml.
140. Steven Millward, "Tencent's Biggest Investments of 2015," *Tech in Asia*, December 23, 2015, accessed February 16, 2017, www.techinasia.com/tencent-startups-invested-acquired-2015.
141. Donny Kwok, "China's AVIC, CITIC, Others Inject $850 Million to Fund Tencent's Supercell Purchase," *Reuters*, October 17, 2016, accessed February 16, 2017, www.reuters.com/article/us-supercell-m-a-tencent-holdings-idUSKBN12H0A8.
142. "History," *WeBank*, August 31, 2016, www.webank.com/aboutus/about.html.
143. Gabriel Wildau, "Tencent Launches China's First Online-Only Bank," *Financial Times*, January 5, 2015, accessed August 31, 2016, www.ft.com/cms/s/0/ccc5a6dc-9488-11e4-82c7-00144feabdc0.html#axzz4J7B9TbU6.
144. Michele Chandler, "Alibaba and Tencent Extend Their Rivalry to Banking Business," *Investor's Business Daily*, February 10, 2015, A04.
145. Tencent, Annual Report, 2011, 146.
146. Jonathan Landreth, "China's Internet Titan Tencent Invests $69 Million in Film Studio Huayi Brothers," *Hollywoodreporter.com*, October 20, 2011, www.hollywoodreporter.com.
147. Meng Yang, "yijia shougou Huayi Xiongdi Tengxun jinjun yingshi quan buchaqian" 溢价收购华谊兄弟 腾讯进军影视圈"不差钱" [Tencent Invested in Huayi Brothers with a Premium Price], *Securities Daily* 证券日报, May 12, 2011, 2.
148. "Annual Report 2011," *Huayi Brothers Media Corporation*, 64, accessed August 30, 2016, www.huayimedia.com; Clarence Tsui, "Chinese Tech Tycoon Jack Ma Reduces Stake in Film Studio Huayi Brothers," *Hollywood reporter.com*, June 6, 2013, accessed August 30, 2016, www.hollywoodreporter.com/news/jack-ma-reduces-stake-huayi-563849.
149. Tencent, Annual Report, 2011, 146.
150. Ibid., 189.
151. Sophie Yu, "ChinaVision to Pay HK$2b for China Entertainment," *South China Morning Post*, October 24, 2011, 4.
152. Ibid.
153. Alibaba Pictures Group Ltd., Annual Report, 2014, 4.
154. Patrick Frater, "China's Tencent Hatches Penguin Pictures," *Variety*, September 11, 2015, accessed March 19, 2017, http://variety.com/2015/film/asia/chinas-tencent-hatches-penguin-pictures-1201591001/.

155. IMDB, "With Tencent Pictures," n.d., accessed January 10, 2019, www.imdb.com/search/title?companies=co0562497.
156. Kwok, "China's AVIC, CITIC, Others Inject $850 Million to Fund Tencent's Supercell Purchase."
157. McChesney, *Digital Disconnect*, 132.
158. Ibid.
159. Xiaobo Wu, *Biography of Tencent* (Zhejiang, China: Zhejiang University Press, 2016), 259–72; Longfei Su, "Tengxun 530 yi de binggou weikou ruhe yangcheng" 腾讯，530亿的并购胃口如何养成 [Tencent's $8.63 billion (RMB 53 billion) investments], *Xin Caifu* 新财富, August 22, 2014, accessed February 16, 2017, http://finance.ifeng.com/a/20140822/12978170_0.shtml.

3 Political Profile

The basic political features—that is, the ownership and control—of Tencent are delved into in this chapter, from looking at the backgrounds of company's founders, aiming to reveal these people's connections to each other and possibly to other state and business actors, to detailing Tencent's ownership and managerial profiles, which show the China-based Internet company's substantial transnational characteristics and linkages, and, to giving special attention to Tencent's primary institutional stakeholder, the South Africa-based media conglomerate Naspers. Tencent has benefited enormously from this close relationship, through which the company is able to extend its global reach via Naspers' worldwide network. Also examined are Tencent's political economic influences as other aspects of its profile. Tencent has become a significant player in the global digital industry through portfolio investments.

Ma Huateng Before Tencent

Ma Huateng's life, family, and education before he established Tencent exerted strong influences on his career as well as the company's development.

Ma Huateng was born in 1971 to a relatively well-off family. Both of his parents worked at the local bureau of China's Maritime Safety Administration in Hainan Province, where Ma Huateng spent his childhood. His father, Ma Chenshu, originally from Chaoshan, Guangdong, rose from an accountant post all the way to deputy chief of the bureau. Ma Huateng's sister, Ma Jiannan, is four years older than he is. At the time when Hainan Province was a vast rural area literally disconnected from the Chinese mainland, Ma's parents tried to give their children a good education with science magazines and books.[1] Ma was said to have developed a strong interest in astronomy thanks to those science books.[2] In 1984 the family moved to Shenzhen in Mainland China at the border with Hong Kong, where Ma Chenshu started working at the Shenzhen Oceanus Group—the first ferry-service operator in Shenzhen—as the head of its accounting department.[3] This was four years after Shenzhen was established as the special economic zone (SEZ) and a time when the city experienced rapid development as an import and export hub. Eventually, Ma Chenshu became the vice president of Shenzhen Yantian Port Group, a state-owned logistics and chain company, and was elected a member on the company's board of directors in 1997.[4] Upon their moving to Shenzhen, Ma Huateng attended Shenzhen Middle School, where he made friends with Chen Yidan, Zhang Zhidong, and Xu Chenye—who all later were the cofounders of Tencent.[5] His sister, Ma Jiannan, would later work at Shenzhen Telecom, which would provide potential connections with the government's telecom and Internet personnel.

College was also an important influence on Ma. The Ministry of Education and Ministry of Culture had participated actively in the process of building China's information superhighway by integrating Internet and information technologies into their ministerial networks. Consequently at the same time, disciplines like computer science, electronic engineering, and other related subjects became the number one choice for Chinese college students to pursue their degrees in. Ma Huateng and his friends were no exception. In 1989 Ma entered Shenzhen University, where he became classmates again with Zhang and Xu, all computer science majors in the electrical engineering department. Ma and Xu became roommates.[6] Another middle school friend, Chen Yidan, studied chemistry in the same college. Ma's time in Shenzhen University was far-reaching, because not only had he formed strong bonds with these people but also discovered and nourished an interest in computer programming.[7] It was also in a time that the nation was in urgent need of talent in the ICT industry. After graduation in 1993, Ma went to work as a software engineer at Runxun, a telecommunication company, at that time primarily running paging services.[8]

During those years at Runxun, Ma spent much of his spare time on CFido, the Chinese FidoNet, a self-organized bulletin-board system a group of Chinese computer and software experts ran, and the fans and experts discussed software development and technical solutions, among other subjects. Many of these people later became the industry leaders. Ma discovered huge excitement in communicating with other computer fans and established his own space—Ponysoft—on CFido.[9] As Lin Jun and Zhang Yuzhou's biography-like book on Ma and Tencent documented,

> Ma Huateng got to know many friends on CFido who later became big names in China's high-tech and Internet industry. They formed a close network. One of these people was Ding Lei, founder and CEO of NetEase, also known by the name of their flagship website 163.com. Ma himself mentioned many times in interviews that Ding was one of his good friends with whom he drank beer and shared ups and downs

> in early stages of their businesses. It was the success of Ding's 163.com that tremendously inspired Ma and his decision to start his own business.[10]

The social and cultural environment of Shenzhen, Ma's family, and college education contributed to his growth as both a computer engineer and entrepreneur and led to the idea of launching a company.[11] Wu Xiaobo, in a more recent account of Tencent, cited the anecdote that the name of the company, which pronounced Teng Xun in mandarin, came from a combination of Ma's name "Teng" and the previous company he worked for "Xun".

Owners and Managers

Capital stands to be the crucial factor that enables or constrains a company's growth in any industry, and it is especially true in the Internet industry. In order to cover the large expenses incurred in obtaining and maintaining a critical mass in operations and for customers, a corporation needs a large amount of capital in a relatively short period of time to maintain the servers, systems, and platforms.[12] Essential to understanding "who has power to make decisions and who benefits from these decisions," the issue of ownership and control lies at the center in many scholarly studies on the political economy of communication industries.[13] In what ways and from whom, then, had Tencent secured enough funds for its growth? Who had ownership and control of the company? Clarifying these questions helps to specify its political structure, which, in turn, is fundamental for related issues, such as profit strategy and diversification. This section aims to answer these questions by tracing how ownership and control evolved along Tencent's continuing development and what factors and players contributed to this process. The company's political profile would show that Tencent was only partly Chinese at birth. The company's growth was deeply intertwined with the expansion of transnational capital into China.

Investors Before Tencent's IPO

As mentioned in Chapter 2, Tencent's founders each put in a different amount of money to make up the company's registered capital. A golden rule in the Internet industry is to "get big fast."[14] It is crucial for Internet companies to accumulate sufficient capital quickly so that they are able to occupy a certain market and expand, as well.[15] Tencent upon its founding in 1998 immediately encountered the economic downturn in Southeast Asia and the bursting of the Internet bubble in North America that struck the entire global tech industry. These events led to trouble raising money from investors. Near the end of 1999, after unsuccessful attempts to sell its

QQ service to local investors in Shenzhen, including Shenzhen Electronics Group, Shenzhen Telecom, and 21cn.com—a subsidiary of China Telecom, Tencent was hardly surviving.[16]

No domestic enterprise or bank was willing to either buy or fund Tencent, so the company sought investments from foreign venture capitalists (VC). It first contacted IDG Ventures China, the Chinese branch of the U.S.-based venture investor International Data Group (IDG).[17] Since the 1980s, IDG had established businesses in China, including publishing *China Computerworld*.[18] IDG Ventures China, founded in 1993, was one of the earliest firms to bring foreign VC into China.[19] Focusing on China's technology industry, IDG Ventures China invested in more than a dozen Chinese technology companies, including Sohu, Soufun, and Ctrip, before it connected with Tencent in 2000.[20] IDG Ventures China was renamed IDG Capital Partners in 2009 and later IDG Capital. By 2018 it had made investments in more than 750 companies in China.[21]

While in negotiation with IDG Venture China, Tencent also approached the Hong Kong telecom giant PCCW.[22] Shortly after the return of Hong Kong to China in 1997, PCCW started seeking opportunities to enter the mainland telecom and Internet markets. In 1999 it participated in Sina's Series C fund-raising with six other companies: Dell as the lead investor, Creative Technology Marketing and Design, SoftBank, Sumitomo Corporation, Trend Micro, and United Overseas Bank for a total amount of $60 million.[23]

Ma Huateng and his colleagues drafted a business plan for IDG Venture China and PCCW, considering two major issues: how much money Tencent would need to survive in the next year and how large a stake Tencent would allow the outside investors to hold.[24] After looking at the budget for buying equipment, maintaining services, and paying employees, Ma put the company's assessed value at $5.5 million.[25] The core founders needed to hold majority positions, and so in the final contract, they asked for $1.1 million from each investor, which made the company's ownership structure in 2000, as 60 percent of the shares held by the founders, 20 percent by IDG Venture China, and 20 percent by PCCW.[26] The deal with PCCW was through one of its wholly owned subsidiaries, Millennium Vocal Limited.[27] While the founding members possessed majority control of the company, this first round of VC investments inserted transnational elements into Tencent.

Neither IDG Venture China's nor PCCW's investments lasted long. Immediately after Tencent signed the deal with them, the global Internet industry entered its winter in the spring of 2000. The dot-com crash started from the sharp fall of the stock prices of U.S. Internet companies, including Yahoo, Cisco, and Amazon, and quickly spread to other parts of the world.[28] Those Chinese Internet companies listed on the NASDAQ board, such as Sina, Sohu, and NetEase, were near the edge of vanishing in days. Tencent was not spared, either. The crash was combined with the problem in Tencent itself. In spite of QQ's popularity, Tencent was not yet able to find a way to monetize its products. Throughout 2000 Tencent put money into maintaining the software's server without much monetary return from users. It was not until 2001 when the company started working with telecom carriers to launch Mobile QQ that QQ was able to contribute positively to Tencent's spreadsheet. By the end of 2000, Tencent was short of money again and would count on a $2 million loan from IDG Venture China and PCCW.[29] At the same time, both investors were actively looking for buyers who would like to take over their shares in Tencent and allow them to exit.

In early 2001 the South Africa media corporation Myriad International Holdings (MIH), whose parent company is Naspers Ltd., approached Tencent to initiate an investment. MIH reached the deal with Tencent to buy all the 20 percent shares held by PCCW and a portion of IDG Venture China's shares, 12.8 percent.[30] By 2001 Tencent execs continued to own a majority 60 percent of the company, with MIH being the second-largest holder with 32.8 percent shares, and IDG Venture China with 7.2 percent. In 2002 MIH bought an additional 13.5 percent from Tencent execs, for a total of 46.3 percent control,[31] and the Tencent team held a majority of 46.5 percent control. From 2002 to 2004, a set of transactions by Tencent, MIH, and IDG eventually left Tencent and MIH each holding 50 percent of the company in 2003, which was the capital structure before Tencent's IPO.[32]

MIH is a wholly owned subsidiary of Naspers Ltd., a South Africa media conglomerate with a complex layout of businesses (discussed in-depth in a later section). Aside from its dominance in South Africa TV, online video, and publishing markets, Naspers had expanded over the years to South Asia, Russia, Eastern and Central Europe, and Latin America. Besides Tencent, Naspers had stakes in other Chinese media companies, including the Beijing Youth Daily, Xinan Media, and Titan Media. Tencent, nonetheless, composed one of Naspers's largest annual income sections. The person who worked on the Naspers-Tencent transaction was David A.M. Wallerstein, vice president of MIH's China business development sector exploring business opportunities for MIH. In 2001 Wallerstein, who is a longtime consultant in China's telecommunications and IT industries, joined Tencent's senior management, later became senior executive vice president, and is now Tencent's chief exploration officer primarily responsible for Tencent's overseas investments.[33] While no official documentation discloses the negotiation process between Tencent and Naspers or explains why and how Naspers came to the decision to invest in Tencent, Charles St. Leger Searle, CEO of Naspers Internet Listed Assets and on Tencent's board of directors, relates that what made Tencent attractive was the "number of users and the 'stickiness' of their instant messaging service."[34] Referred to as a "bet" by a *Financial Times* story, the investment transformed "Naspers from an ageing local print business into Africa's biggest media company."[35] By August 2016, as a *Seeking Alpha* report suggests, the value of Naspers's stake in Tencent—which was worth approximately $83 billion—outpaced Naspers's own market capitalization of $73 billion, based on its closing price on August 19, 2016.[36]

In April 2004, prior to Tencent's IPO, the founders of the company and MIH entered into a three-year shareholders' agreement, which set the tone for how they were about to control the company:

> Each Founder and MIH will vote their Shares so that the Board and any board of directors of a subsidiary in which the Company holds more than half of the equity interests (the "Equity Controlled Subsidiaries") will have an equal number of directors nominated by the Founders and MIH, respectively. They will also take all necessary action within their respective authority to ensure that the Directors so nominated constitute the majority of the Board and the sole directors of each Equity Controlled Subsidiary.[37]

As stated in the agreement, the founders of Tencent would nominate the chief executive officer, and MIH would name the chief financial officer. Other than appointing its own financial director, however, Naspers did not seem to interfere much in Tencent's managing or decision-making process, according to another member from Naspers sitting on Tencent's board, Antonie Andries Roux.[38] In an interview with *Bloomberg*, Roux said, "We don't micromanage these guys."[39]

Ownership and Managing Structures

Before going into the specific ownership structure, a review of the regulations of the Hong Kong Stock Exchange (HKSE) would be helpful to understand the parameters of revealing substantial owners. According to HKSE, "substantial shareholders are required to disclose interests in shares of listed corporations. Directors and chief executives of a listed corporation are required to disclose interests in shares and debentures of the listed corporation and its associated corporations." The term "substantial shareholders" is defined as "individuals and corporations who are interested in 5 percent or more of any class of voting shares in a listed corporation" must disclose their interests, and short positions, in voting shares of the listed corporation.[40] As the IPO allowed Tencent to raise money from public shareholders and thus diluted the shares held by Tencent and MIH, the company's shareholding structure immediately upon its IPO took the form shown in Figure 3.1. Of the 30.73 percent shares owned by Tencent's core founders, Ma held 14.43 percent and Zhang 6.43 percent.[41]

In 2005 ABSA Bank Ltd., a wholly owned subsidiary bank of the Barclays Africa Group, started holding 10.46 percent security interest in Tencent, the arrangement was a result of deals made between ABSA and Naspers.[42] As a South Africa financial institution, ABSA launched free ISP services in 2001, which resulted in a decrease of Naspers's Internet subscribers.[43] In March 2005 MultiChoice Africa Ltd., a Naspers wholly owned subsidiary that operates the sub-Saharan pay-television businesses, entered into an agreement with ABSA for a revolving-loan facility.[44] As part of the deal, the Naspers Group "pledged 110,474,041 shares in United Broadcasting Public Company Limited (UBC) and 185,000,000 shares in Tencent Holdings Limited as security for the loan facility."[45] During the term of the loan agreement, from 2005 to March 3, 2010, 185,000,000 shares of Tencent were pledged to ABSA, or approximately 10 percent of Tencent, while the exact number varied year by year.[46]

In 2010 JPMorgan Chase and Co. acquired 5,655,577 shares as beneficial owner, 34,888,700 as investment manager, and 51,354,694 as custodian corporation or approved lending agent, which altogether added up

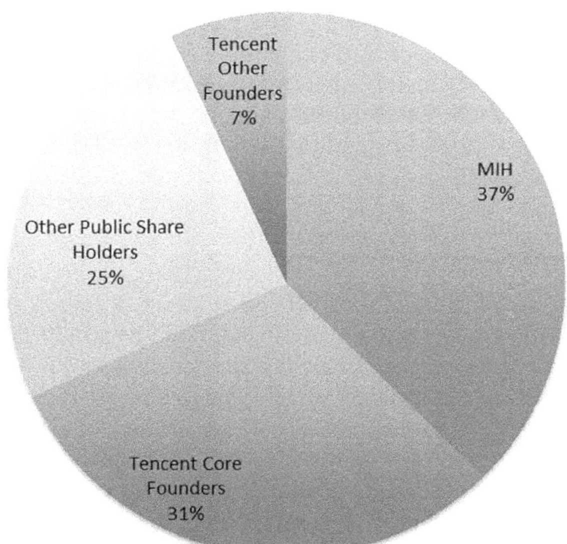

Figure 3.1 Tencent's Shareholding Structure Immediately After IPO

Source: Tencent, Prospectus.

to 5.01 percent of Tencent's issued share capital.[47] No available document discloses in what ways the bank became interested in Tencent and to what extent it exerted control over Tencent's operation. As sociologist Maurice Zeitlin observed in 1974, large corporations heavily depended on a small number of large banks that dominated the capital market; the connection between Tencent and JPMorgan Chase attests to the "actual coalescence of financial and industrial capital."[48] Investment banks in modern merger-and-acquisition deals take advantage of their "access to privileged information" and, hence, possess a level of corporate control, a 2009 study found.[49] Internet companies increasingly rely on banks, as these companies were more likely to use international financing to raise money regardless of currencies, a 2014 study said.[50] These all suggest that the interconnection between financial institutions and the Internet industry was a necessary step to help the Internet industry access the global capital market. JPMorgan Chase remained a substantial shareholder of Tencent, and its stakes increased to an approximate 7.25 percent shareholding till December 2017.[51]

Zhang Zhidong, a cofounder and the company's technology chief, retired from Tencent in September 2014 and was no longer disclosed as a substantial shareholder. He is now "the Advisor Emeritus of the Company and Honorary Dean of Tencent Academy."[52] As of 2018, the major shareholders with over 5 percent long position shares were MIH with 33.10 percent and Ma Huateng, 8.61 percent.[53]

Table 3.1 Tencent's Major Shareholders, 2004–18

Year	*Shareholder*				
	MIH QQ (BVI)	*Ma Huateng*	*Zhang Zhidong*	*ABSA*	*JPMorgan Chase*
2004	35.71	13.74	6.12		
2005	35.62	13.14	5.26	10.46	
2006	35.64	13.10	5.04	10.46	
2007	35.24	12.81	4.64	10.34	
2008	35.08	11.85	4.29	10.30	
2009	34.65	11.54	3.75	10.17	
2010	34.33	11.16	3.66	10.08	5.01
2011	34.26	10.32	3.63		(unspecified)
2012	34.01	10.25	3.56		(unspecified)
2013	33.85	10.20	3.49		5.02
2014	33.63	9.86			6.27
2015	33.51	9.10			6.24
2016	33.25	8.73			5.97
2017	33.17	8.63			7.25
2018	33.10	8.61			

Sources: Tencent, Annual Reports, 2004–18 (revenue year-end of December 31).

Table 3.2 Tencent's Board of Directors, 2004–18

Board Member	*Position*	*Affiliation*	*Ties to Tencent or Ma Huateng*
Jacobus Petrus Bekker (appointed November 14, 2012)	Non-executive director	Managing director, CEO, Naspers	—
Iain Ferguson Bruce	Independent non-executive director	Former senior partner KPMG, former chairman KPMG Asia Pacific	—
Lau Chi Ping Martin (appointed March 21, 2007)	Executive director	Chief strategy and investment officer, Tencent (since February 2005); president, Tencent (since February 2006)	Former chief operating officer Goldman Sachs (Asia), Telecom, Media and Technology Group. Goldman Sachs team for Tencent IPO
Li Dong Sheng	Independent non-executive director	chairman, CEO, TCL	—
Ma Huateng	Chairman, executive director	CEO, Tencent	Core founder
Antonie Andries Roux (deceased June 24, 2012)	Non-executive director	CEO, Internet operations, MIH group	—
Charles St. Leger Searle	Non-executive director	Director of corporate development, MIH group in Asia	—
Ian Charles Stone	Independent non-executive director	Consultant, PCCW; director, CEO, UK Broadband	—
Yang Siu Shun (appointed July 1, 2016)	Independent non-executive director	Chairman and principal partner of PWC Hong Kong, executive chairman and principal partner of PWC Chinese Mainland, independent non-executive director of Industrial and Commercial Bank of China Limited	—
Zhang Zhidong (retired March 20, 2014)	Executive director	Chief technology officer, Tencent	Core founder

Sources: Tencent, Annual Reports, 2004–18 (revenue year-end of December 31).

Another important indicator of a company's control is the composition of the board of directors. For major media corporations, this makeup suggests a strong interdependency between corporations and their board members.[54] Board members are selected based on the resources they can bring to a corporation from their ties to "other major industrial firms, banks, think tanks, law firms, business policy-planning groups, and foundations."[55] In a study of the boards of directors of one hundred media corporations, the author warns that the interlocking directorships might cause conflicts of interests in the flow of information and expression.[56] For Tencent, its board of directors was mostly composed of the core founders and those who had prior connections to MIH and Naspers. In addition, Martin Lau, the former executive director at Goldman Sachs (Asia), who worked on Tencent's IPO project, joined Tencent in 2005 as the chief strategy and investment officer. He has been the president of the company since 2006 and an executive director of the board since 2007.[57]

Of the board members listed in Table 3.2, except for the deceased Roux and the retired Zhang, all are active board members as of early 2019. Tencent's directors are internationally connected rather than exclusively Chinese.

In the Jungle of Naspers

Tencent's largest institutional stakeholder is a South Africa-based media conglomerate, Naspers. A preliminary political economy profile of Naspers, with respect to its ownership role in Tencent, will illuminate Tencent's connection with Naspers as an aspect of Tencent's political profile and transnational expansion.

Naspers was founded in 1915. Starting out as a Dutch-language newspaper company in South Africa, it now has become a transnational multimedia conglomerate with businesses primarily in the Internet, entertainment, and technology investments across the globe.[58] Naspers is publicly listed on the Johannesburg Stock Exchange (JSE) and on the London Stock Exchange (LSE) for American Depository Shares (ADSs), which would allow international investors to buy and sell Naspers securities either through the JSE or LSE.[59] In an annual report, the company claims to be one of the leading technology investors in the world:

> Over the decades we have transformed thoroughly. Starting as a single-country newspaper group, we risked becoming an early investor in pay television and mobile telephony in one country. Then we grew into a video-entertainment leader and a major global consumer internet and ecommerce group in over 130 countries. Looking at our business as a whole on an economic interest basis and including our share

> of associates and joint ventures, almost 60% of our revenues are now derived from internet and ecommerce segments. Below 30% of our revenues are sourced in South Africa.[60]

As of March 2018, Naspers achieved an annual revenue of $20.1 billion, of which $15.9 billion came from Internet businesses, $3.7 billion from video entertainment, and $374 million from the media sector.[61]

Geographically, Naspers has investments as its associate companies or joint ventures with fifty-one corporations around the world. Seven of them are in Asia, eleven in the Middle East and Africa, four in Latin America, one in North America, and five in Central and Eastern Europe; another twelve of the group companies are operating globally.[62] This corresponds with Naspers's strategic plan in focusing on BRICSA, a group of the major emerging national economies of Brazil, Russia, India, China, and the company refers to SA as sub-Sahara Africa.

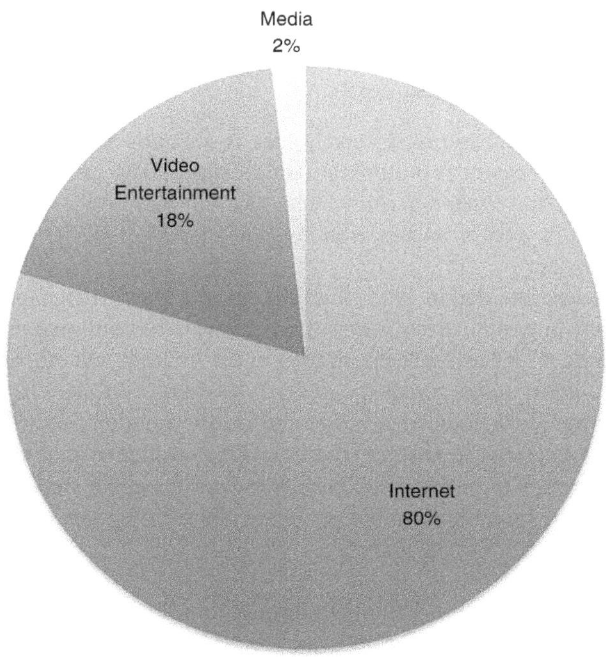

Figure 3.2 Naspers 2018 Revenue by Segment

Source: Naspers's annual financial statements for the year ended March 31, 2018.

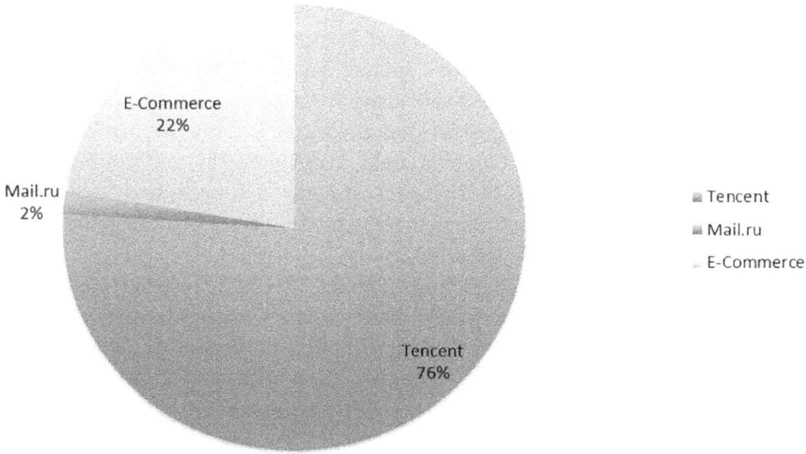

Figure 3.3 Naspers 2018 Revenue in Internet Segment

Source: Naspers's annual financial statements for the year ended March 31, 2018.

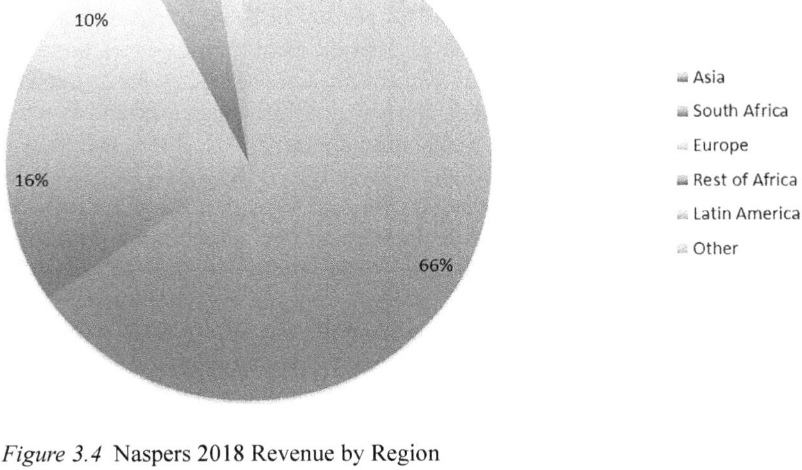

Figure 3.4 Naspers 2018 Revenue by Region

Source: Naspers's annual financial statements for the year ended March 31, 2018.

As of 2018, Tencent is one of the two significant profit generators for Naspers Group, contributing $9.8 billion to Naspers's spreadsheet in March 2018, which was 76 percent of its Internet segment and 49 percent of its overall revenue.[63] The other heavyweight interest is in a leading Russian Internet group, Mail.ru, in which Naspers's wholly owned subsidiary MIH holds a 28.4 percent equity interest.[64] Mail.ru runs "the largest Russian portal, the leading Russian language social networks (VKontakte, Odnoklassniki, and My World) and the country's largest online-game business."[65] These investments in Tencent and Mail.ru, as well as some other unlisted companies, reflect a development strategy to focus on the burgeoning markets in BRICSA.[66]

Aside from Tencent, Naspers had invested in China in print media, as well. As early as 2002, Naspers held interests in a Chinese-language sports portal, SportsCn, with an 87.66 percent of equity interest as of June 2004.[67] In 2004 when Beijing Media Corporation, the operator of *Beijing Youth Daily*, launched an IPO on the HKSE, MIH acquired 9.9 percent interest in the noneditorial segment of the company.[68] This was possible due to the "dual-track ownership" system in China's print-media industry, where the business operation and news production were separated and could be owned by different entities.[69] To be sure, this means that the content-production department must be state-owned still, but private investments are allowed in the noneditorial sectors, such as the advertising, marketing, sales, and PR departments.[70] In August 2006 Naspers purchased a 20 percent equity interest in a Changsha, Hunan-based leading Chinese sports publisher, Titan Media.[71] Subsequently, the Chinese-language sports magazines *Allsports*, *Golf Digest*, *Outside*, *Slam*, *Soccer Weekly*, and *Yoga*—all published by Titan Media—became part of Naspers's global media family.[72] The stake in Titan Media was increased to a 37.4 percent in 2008.[73] In 2009 Naspers started investing in an Anhui Province-based local evening-news group—Xin'an Media Co. Ltd.—with 37 percent interest in it.[74] But due to a tough and declining print-media market, Naspers gradually decreased and eventually dropped its investment in these corporations in 2011, 2013, and 2014.[75]

As Tencent's major institutional stakeholder, MIH and, thus, Naspers maintain a certain level of control on Tencent through a set of agreements that conditions their relationship. First, with two directors on Tencent's board from MIH—Roux and Searle—MIH retains the right to nominate Tencent's chief financial officer.[76] Second, Tencent and MIH have entered a series of license agreements that grant MIH and its affiliates a sole and exclusive license to use Tencent's proprietary technology and intellectual property in Indonesia, Thailand, Greece, Cyprus, and South Africa. Another supplemental agreement also allows MIH and the MIH operators to use Tencent's trademarks and other intellectual property when carrying on the Internet-related business for up to 15 years.[77] But no document indicates that Naspers dictates Tencent's autonomous operations.

On the other hand, with its wide reach in global media industries, Naspers also has assisted with Tencent's transnational expansion. A certain portion of Tencent's foreign investments, mostly joint ventures and acquisitions, was made through the Naspers connection.

In June 2008 Tencent and Naspers's India-based wholly owned subsidiary MIH India Global Internet agreed to allow Tencent to possess up to nearly 50 percent of the MIH India's shares. In exchange, Tencent granted licenses to MIH India for the use of certain of Tencent's services.[78] Tencent excised its options by subsequently obtaining a minority stake of 6 percent in December 2008 and 4 percent in March 2009.[79] As Tencent's stakes in MIH India were through an internal transfer from Naspers, MIH India after the transaction became a joint venture between Tencent and Naspers. In October 2013 Naspers and Tencent restructured their Indian businesses. MIH India Global's businesses were split into two parts: social network and e-commerce, with Tencent holding 80.1 percent and 19.9 percent interest in the two, respectively. The MIH Group took the remaining 19.9 percent of social network and 80.1 percent of e-commerce.[80]

In April 2010 Tencent announced a $300 million investment in Digital Sky Technologies Ltd., a leading Internet company in the Russian-speaking and Eastern European markets, which was renamed Mail.ru in October 2010.[81] The transaction gave Tencent 11.46 percent economic interest and 0.52 percent voting interest in the Russian Internet company, while Naspers, a longtime investor in Mail.ru through MIH, held 29.1 percent economic interest and 35 percent voting power.[82]

In October 2010 Tencent purchased 49.92 percent equity interest of Sanook.com, an Internet-service company in Thailand, from MIH with $10.501 million (RMB 71.143 million).[83] In October 2013 the Thai operation in cooperation with MIH was also reorganized and the Thai business was separated into two categories of social network and e-commerce; Tencent held 99.2 percent of the social-network business, with no interest in the e-commerce business, and MIH held the e-commerce sector but no interest in the other.[84] With respect to the social-network sector, Tencent's focus was primarily on collaborating with the leading Internet service provider in Thailand—Sanook—to integrate its services into WeChat's mobile messaging platform.[85]

On January 19, 2012, Tencent announced an agreement to buy 320,722 shares, for $26.950 million (RMB 169.567 million), of Level Up! International Holdings Limited, a Singapore-incorporated online-game and game-magazine publishing company, wholly owned by MIH LatAm Holdings, a subsidiary of Naspers.[86] The acquisition, completed in July 2012, comprised 49 percent of Level Up's issued share capital.[87] In October 2013 Tencent acquired an additional 18 percent of Level Up shares from MIH LatAm, making Tencent's stake in Level Up a total of 67 percent.[88] According to

Tencent's disclosure, the investment in Level Up, as a dominant game publisher and operator in Brazil and the Philippines, was to consolidate Tencent's strategy in developing online games in emerging markets.[89] In March 2014, however, the entire entity of Level Up was acquired by a Thailand-based online game and entertainment company, Asiasoft.[90]

To summarize, Tencent, as it contributes greatly to the Naspers empire's balance sheet, also benefited from Naspers's worldwide outreach by extending Tencent's own businesses to Eastern Europe, Russia, and South and Southeast Asia. Through this relation with Naspers, Tencent is becoming a more prominent global Internet company.

From Investee to Investor

As the company grew and matured, Tencent started extending its own control through massive investments as a venture capitalist (VC). As a 2013 *Wall Street Journal* article reports, Tencent "has sought for years to gain a toehold in the U.S." and lately has been "one of the [Silicon] Valley's most aggressive players."[91] Tencent's brief history as a VC investor is another aspect of its control and power.

In January 2011 Tencent established its Tencent Collaboration Fund, with an initial funding of $750 million (RMB 5 billion), to support "innovative companies in Internet industry."[92] The fund operated as a VC investor that engaged—by itself or in partnerships—in seed, early-stage venture, and later-stage venture investments.[93] According to a company report, the businesses were primarily focused on "online gaming, social network sites (SNS), mobile Internet, e-commerce and new media."[94] In June 2011, only half a year after the creation of the fund, Tencent revealed a plan to further invest $1.5 billion (RMB 10 billion).[95] Up to March 2017, three of its successful and high-profile cases include investments in Huayi Brothers Media Group, a Chinese film production and distribution giant; Kaixin001, a social-media network targeted at urban, white-collar workers; and Didi Chuxing, China's leading ridesharing and "mobile transportation platform."[96]

In the meantime, Tencent's VC was flowing from China to the United States' technology hub, Silicon Valley. Tencent's U.S. investment arm, based in Palo Alto, California, was led by Tencent's Wallerstein, chief eXploration officer (CXO) and senior executive vice president. As mentioned earlier, Wallerstein used to work for Naspers and was one of the key figures to make Naspers's deal with Tencent happen in 2000. He joined Tencent in 2001 and ever since has been in charge of exploring the company's international prospects.[97] According to a *Wall Street Journal*'s report, Wallerstein and his colleagues, described by a local entrepreneur as "well-connected," were regular guests at the offices of venture capitalists and industry events from the technology and investing industries.[98]

In 2012 Tencent became partners with VC firms, including Andreessen Horowitz and SV Angel, and began co-investing in the American start-ups these investors put chips in.[99] According to a *CNN* report, Tencent has invested in more than 300 start-ups in the past ten years, covering a wide range, from digital games and social media to mobile applications and e-commerce.[100] The highlights of these deals include the investments in Fab and Snapchat. In 2013 Tencent made a $150 million investment in the New York-based design website Fab, which gave Tencent a seat on Fab's board of directors.[101] Also in the same year, Tencent took part as an unrevealed minority participant in a $60 million investment in Snapchat led by Institutional Venture Partners.[102] Ironically and interestingly, Tencent's biggest competitor in China—Alibaba—also became an investor in Snapchat in 2015 when it poured $200 million into Snapchat's Series E funding round.[103] A more recent high-profile investment took place in early 2017 when Tencent bought a 5 percent stake in Elon Musk's Tesla for $1.8 billion.[104]

Tencent's VC investment was, however, not bound to the United States. In 2015 Tencent made a few separate investments in the Canadian mobile messaging app Kik and Indian health-care technology start-up Practo, among others. Valuing the Canadian start-up of mobile messaging application at $1 billion, Tencent made a $50 million investment in Kik Interactive Inc.[105] On the other side of the world, the Indian online health-care platform Practo received a $90 million funding from Tencent.[106] Together with Tencent were other venture capitalists "Google Capital, Sofina, Sequoia India, Altimeter Capital, Matrix Partners, Sequoia Capital Global Equities and Russian billionaire Yuri Milner."[107] It has become apparent that VC investment is now a new vehicle of corporate control and expansion through large units of Internet capital.

Conclusion

Tencent's emergence from a small local company to a global digital giant can be characterized by a number of interconnected elements. First and foremost, arguably, was the opening up of the domestic market to foreign capital in various forms and, especially, the participation of transnational VC in the Internet industry that supported Tencent's seed funding as well as financed its continual expansion. This further warrants the established argument from the previous chapter that China's Internet industry grew out of a time of political-economic changes when domestic needs for capitalist reproduction met the transnational wants for enlarging market investments.

Looking at its ownership and governance shows that Tencent is a China-based transnational Internet company whose political economy means much more than the company as an isolated organization unit. Unveiling Tencent's connection with its primary institutional holder, Naspers, as well as Tencent's portfolio investments as an extension of its corporate control, further demonstrates the intertwined and dialectical relations between China's Internet industry and the transitional capitalist system.[108]

In its current stage of development, Tencent seeks to become an influential player in the field on its own through extending corporate and capital control to other digital companies. While traditional PEC studies also emphasize the corporate-government relations and, especially, corporate lobbying efforts, in this case, not much documentation reveals Tencent's government relations, except for the known fact that Ma Huateng is a deputy to the Thirteenth National People's Congress through which he could share thoughts and suggestions regarding the "digital China" blueprint.[109]

Notes

1. "Gaosu ni buzhidao de gushi: Xiao qie QQ shi zheyang zhangda de" 告诉你不知道的故事: "小企鹅" QQ 是这样长大的 [An untold story: How the tiny penguin QQ grows], *Chaoshan Businessman* 3, no. 1 (2010), accessed August 15, 2016, http://cs.dahuawang.com/view.asp?newsno=589; X. Wu, *Biography of Tencent*, chap. 1.
2. X. Wu, *Biography of Tencent*, chap. 1.
3. Jun Lin and Yuezhou Zhang, *"Ma Huateng de Tengxun Diguo"* 马化腾的腾讯帝国 *[Ma Huateng's Tencent Empire]* (Beijing: China Citic Press, 2009), 17.
4. Ibid.
5. X. Wu, *Biography of Tencent*, 6–8.
6. Ibid., 9–12.
7. Ibid.
8. Lin and Zhang, *Ma Huateng de Tengxun Diguo*, 8–11.
9. Ibid., 25–28; X. Wu, *Biography of Tencent*, 14–17.
10. Lin and Zhang, *Ma Huateng de Tengxun Diguo*, 27–28. Ding Lei was also known as William Ding.
11. X. Wu, *Biography of Tencent*, 20–23.
12. Carl Shapiro and Hai R. Varian, *Information Rules: A Strategic Guide to the Network Economy* (Boston: Harvard Business, 1999), pp 280–281; Crain, "The Revolution Will Be Commercialized," pp 14–17.
13. André Sirois and Janet Wasko, "The Political Economy of the Recorded Music Industry: Redefinitions and New Trajectories in the Digital Age," in *The Handbook of Political Economy of Communications*, eds. Janet Wasko, Graham Murdock, and Helena Sousa (Chichester: Wiley-Blackwell, 2011), 331–357.
14. Shapiro and Varian, *Information Rules*, 280.
15. Ibid.
16. X. Wu, *Biography of Tencent*, 50–53.
17. Bruce Einhorn and Brad Stone, "Tencent: March of the Penguins," *Bloomberg Businessweek*, August 4, 2011, accessed August 16, 2015, www.bloomberg.com/bw/magazine/tencent-march-of-the-penguins-08042011.html.
18. Louis Hau, "IDG Goes to China," *Forbes*, August 28, 2006, accessed December 6, 2016, www.forbes.com/2006/08/25/idg-china-magazines-mcgovern-cx_lh_0828idg.html.
19. "About," *IDG Capital*, n.d., accessed December 6, 2016, www.idgvc.com/en; David Cyranoski, "Venture Capitalists Tackle Chinese Hurdles," *Nature* 437,

no. 1087 (2005), doi:10.1038/4371087a, accessed June 17, 2015, www.nature.com/nature/journal/v437/n7062/full/4371087a.html.
20. IDG Capital Partners, "Timeline," *Crunchbase*, accessed December 6, 2016, www.crunchbase.com/organization/idg-capital-partners/timeline#/timeline/index.
21. IDG Capital, "About Us," accessed January 12, 2019, http://en.idgcapital.com/about-us.
22. X. Wu, *Biography of Tencent*, 53–57.
23. Hans Lombardo, "Sina.com Closes $60 Million with Dell as Lead Investor," *InternetNews.com*, November 9, 1999, accessed December 6, 2016, www.internetnews.com/bus-news/article.php/234731/Sinacom+Closes+60+Million+with+Dell+as+Lead+Investor.htm.
24. X. Wu, *Biography of Tencent*, 53–57.
25. Lin and Zhang, *Ma Huateng de Tengxun Diguo*, 68–69.
26. Ibid., 72.
27. "Our History and Structure [Tencent]," *HKEX*, www.hkexnews.hk/listedco/listconews/sehk/2004/0607/0700/EWP113.pdf.
28. David Kleinbard, "The $1.7 Trillion Dot.com Lesson," *CNN Money*, November 9, 2000, accessed November 9, 2016, http://cnnfn.cnn.com/2000/11/09/technology/overview/.
29. X. Wu, *Biography of Tencent*, 60–63.
30. Lin and Zhang, *Ma Huateng de Tengxun Diguo*, 77–78.
31. Ibid.
32. Tencent, Prospectus, 306.
33. Tencent, Annual Report, 2011, 43.
34. Patrick Boehler, "South African Media Group Struck Gold by Taking a Chance on Tencent," *South China Morning Post*, February 21, 2014, accessed December 13, 2016, www.scmp.com/news/china-insider/article/1432550/south-african-publishing-group-struck-gold-taking-chance-tencent.
35. Andrew England, "Naspers Looks Beyond Tencent Success," *Financial Times*, June 27, 2015, accessed December 13, 2016, www.ft.com/content/82e365aa-1984-11e5-a130-2e7db721f996.
36. Kevin Quon, "Why Naspers Is an Undervalued Tech Play on the Developing World," *Seeking Alpha*, August 21, 2016, accessed December 13, 2016, http://seekingalpha.com/article/4001032-naspers-undervalued-tech-play-developing-world; Dana Sanchez, "Naspers Owns a Third of What Is Now China's Most Valuable Company: What This Means for South Africa," *AFK Insider*, September 6, 2016, accessed December 13, 2016, http://afkinsider.com/132392/naspers-owns-a-third-of-what-is-now-chinas-most-valuable-company-what-this-means-for-south-africa/.
37. Tencent, Prospectus, 135.
38. Boehler, "South African Media Group Struck Gold."
39. "Naspers Scours Emerging Markets after Tencent Success," *Bloomberg*, December 14, 2010, accessed December 13, 2016, http://chinese988.blogspot.com/2010_12_12_archive.html.
40. "Shareholding Disclosures," *HKEX News*, n.d., accessed August 16, 2016, http://sdinotice.hkex.com.hk/di/NSSrchMethod.aspx; "Securities and Futures Ordinance Part XV—Disclosure of Interests," *Securities and Futures Commission (Hong Kong)*, n.d., accessed August 16, 2016, www.sfc.hk/web/EN/rule-book/sfo-part-xv-disclosure-of-interests/.
41. Tencent, Prospectus, 74, 134.

42. "Overview," *ABSA*, n.d., accessed December 13, 2016, www.absa.co.za/Absacoza/About-Absa/Absa-Bank/Absa-Overview.
43. Naspers, "Form F-4," *Securities and Exchange Commission*, November 1, 2002, accessed December 13, 2016, www.sec.gov/Archives/edgar/data/1106051/000091205702040648/a2091992zf-4.htm.
44. Naspers, "Form 20-F," *Securities and Exchange Commission*, September 30, 2005, accessed December 13, 2016, www.sec.gov/Archives/edgar/data/1106051/000095015705000630/naspers-20f.htm.
45. Ibid.
46. Tencent, Annual Report, 2005, 32.
47. Ibid., 44.
48. Maurice Zeitlin, "Corporate Ownership and Control: The Large Corporation and the Capitalist Class," *American Journal of Sociology* 79, no. 5 (1974): 1101.
49. Andriy Bodnaruk, Massimo Massa, and Andrei Simonov, "Investment Banks as Insiders and the Market for Corporate Control," *Review of Financial Studies* 22, no. 12 (2009): 4989–5026.
50. Anton Miglo, Zhenting Lee, and Shuting Liang, "Capital Structure of Internet Companies: Case Study," *Journal of Internet Commerce* 13, no. 3–4 (2014): 253–81.
51. Tencent, Interim Report 2016, 79. There was no disclosure of information related to JPMorgan in Tencent's 2011 and 2012 annual reports. However, in the 2012 interim report, JPMorgan was disclosed again as a substantial shareholder with 5 percent in August 2012. Because its shares fell below 5 percent between 2011 and 2012 JPMorgan was not mentioned in these annual reports, but it seems consistent that since 2010 the bank was a Tencent beneficial owner, investment manager, and custodian corporation or approved lending agent.
52. Tencent, "Management Team."
53. Tencent, Annual Report, 2018.
54. Kyun-Tae Han, "Composition of Board of Directors of Major Media Corporations," *Journal of Media Economics* 1, no. 2 (1988): 85–100.
55. Ibid., 85.
56. Ibid., 97.
57. Tencent, Annual Report, 2006, 26.
58. Tewodrow W. Workneh, "Sub-Saharan Africa," in *Global Media Giants*, eds. Benjamin J. Birkinbine, Rodrigo Gomez, and Janet Wasko (New York: Routledge, 2017), 287–311.
59. "ADR Information," *Naspers*, n.d., accessed March 3, 2017, http://cdn.naspers.com/page.html?pageID=29; Workneh, "Sub-Saharan Africa."
60. Naspers, Integrated Annual Report, 2015, 8, accessed September 18, 2016, http://cdn.naspers.com/financial-reporting.html.
61. Naspers, "Annual Financial Results 2018," accessed January 13, 2019, www.naspers.com/getattachment/16c28ce7-76d2-478b-854f-7f246de31d2d/Naspers_Annual_financial_statements_2018.pdf.aspx?lang=en-US.
62. The regions are used according to how the company decides its market locations. "About Naspers," *Naspers*, accessed September 18, 2016, www.naspers.com/about.
63. Naspers, "Summarized Consolidated Financial Results 2016," 5–10, accessed September 18, 2016, www.naspers.com/NaspersPortal/media/Naspers/Pdf/financials/integrated-annual-reports/Naspers-Summarised-consolidated-financial-results.pdf?ext=.pdf.
64. Naspers, Integrated Annual Report, 2018.

65. Naspers, Integrated Annual Report, 2015, 53.
66. Naspers, Annual Report, 2006, 8.
67. Naspers, Annual Report, 2002, 6; Tencent, Prospectus, 136.
68. Naspers, Annual Report, 2006, 37, 92.
69. Shixin Ivy Zhang, *Impact of Globalization on the Local Press in China: A Case Study of the Beijing Youth Daily* (Lanham, MD: Lexington, 2014), 40.
70. Ibid.
71. Naspers, Annual Report, 2007, 42.
72. Ibid., 7.
73. Ibid., 37.
74. Ibid., 108.
75. Ibid., 66; Ibid., 2013, 17; Ibid., 2014.
76. Tencent, Prospectus, 135.
77. Ibid., 137.
78. Tencent, Annual Report, 2008, 95–96.
79. "Naspers Invested Over $10 M in Ibibo in FY10; Goibibo $1M Per Month; Payments Platform?" *Medianama*, September 3, 2010.
80. "Connected Transactions: Restructuring of the Businesses in India and Thailand, Exercise of the Level Up Option," *Tencent*, October 10, 2013, accessed September 18, 2016, www.tencent.com/en-us/news_timeline.html.
81. Mail.ru, Annual Report, 2010, 49.
82. Ibid., 33, 88.
83. Tencent, Annual Report, 2010, 134; "Tencent's Fake Guns Mean Real Money for Global Acquisitions," *Bloomberg News*, November 8, 2010, accessed September 18, 2016, www.bloomberg.com/news/articles/2010-11-09/tencent-s-fake-weapons-fund-2-billion-war-chest-for-overseas-acquisitions.
84. "Connected Transactions."
85. Willis Wee, "The Future of Sanook: Thailand's Largest Web Portal," *Tech in Asia*, April 2, 2013, accessed September 18, 2016, www.techinasia.com/sanook-thailand-largest-web-portal-under-tiwa-york-krittee-manoleehagul.
86. "Connect Transaction: Purchase of Shares of Level Up," *Tencent*, January 19, 2012, accessed September 18, 2016, www.tencent.com/en-us/news_timeline.html.
87. Tencent, Annual Report, 2011, 189; Tencent, Annual Report, 2012, 60.
88. "Connected Transactions."
89. Ibid.
90. Asiasoft, Annual Report, 2014, 139, accessed September 18, 2016, http://as.listedcompany.com/ar.html.
91. Evelyn M. Rusli and Paul Mozur, "China Buys Its Way into Silicon Valley," *Wall Street Journal*, November 4, 2013, accessed March 3, 2017, www.wsj.com/articles/SB10001424052702303843104579171963801529056.
92. "Tencent Sets Up a Collaboration Fund—To Further Advance Its Open Development Strategy in the Internet Industry," press release, *Tencent*, January 24, 2011, accessed March 6, 2017, www.tencent.com/en-us/articles/80085.html. The exchange rate was calculated using X-rates' monthly average in 2011, accessed March 6, 2017, www.x-rates.com/average. The collaboration fund is also referred to as "industry win-win fund," according to "Tencent Industry Win-Win Fund: Investor Details," *Crunchbase*, accessed March 6, 2017, www.crunchbase.com/organization/tencent-industry-win-win-fund#/entity, or as "industrial investment fund," "Company Overview of Tencent Collaboration Fund," *Bloomberg*, accessed March 6, 2017, www.bloomberg.com/research/stocks/private/snapshot.asp?privcapId=127754428. To avoid confusion, I refer to it as "the fund" or "the collaboration fund."

93. "Tencent Industry Win-Win Fund."
94. "Tencent Sets Up a Collaboration Fund."
95. "Tencent Holds Partners Conference and Unveils Plan to Build the Most Successful Open Platform," press release, *Tencent*, June 15, 2011, accessed March 6, 2017, www.tencent.com/en-us/articles/80078.html.
96. "Tencent Industry Win-Win Fund: Timeline," *Crunchbase*, n.d., accessed March 6, 2017, www.crunchbase.com/organization/tencent-industry-win-win-fund/timeline#/timeline/index.
97. Tencent, "Management Team."
98. Evelyn M. Rusli and Paul Mozur, "China Taps Silicon Valley—Homegrown Web Giants Pump Money into U.S. Startups at Lofty Valuations," *Wall Street Journal*, November 5, 2013, B1.
99. "Alibaba vs. Tencent—Comparing the U.S. Investment Activity of the Chinese Internet Giants," *CB Insights*, January 1, 2015, accessed October 25, 2016, www.cbinsights.com/blog/alibaba-tencent-investments/.
100. Sherisse Pham, "Tencent Has Pumped Billions into 300 Companies," *CNN Business*, October 4, 2018, accessed February 24, 2019, www.cnn.com/2018/10/04/tech/tencent-investment-strategy-explained/index.html.
101. Spencer E. Ante and Paul Mozur, "New Funding Values Fab at Over $1 Billion," *Wall Street Journal*, June 19, 2013, accessed October 25, 2016, www.wsj.com/articles/SB10001424127887323836504578553820174945626.
102. Kim-Mai Cutler, "Tencent Was Already a Covert Investor in Snapchat's Last Round," *TechCrunch*, November 20, 2013, accessed October 25, 2016. https://techcrunch.com/2013/11/20/tencent-snapchat/.
103. Scott Cendrowski, "Why Is Alibaba Investing in Snapchat?" *Fortune*, March 12, 2015, accessed October 25, 2016, http://fortune.com/2015/03/12/why-is-alibaba-investing-in-snapchat/.
104. Dana Hull, John Lippert, and Selina Wang, "Tencent Emerges as Musk's China Booster with 5% Tesla Stake," *Bloomberg*, March 28, 2017, accessed February 24, 2019, www.bloomberg.com/news/articles/2017-03-28/tencent-buys-1-8-billion-tesla-stake-ahead-of-musk-s-model-3.
105. David George-Cosh and Douglas MacMillan, "Tencent Invests $50 Million in Messaging App Kik," *Wall Street Journal*, August 18, 2015.
106. Jake Maxwell Watts, "Tencent, Google Capital Invest in Indian Healthcare Startup Practo," *Wall Street Journal*, August 6, 2015, accessed October25,2016,http://blogs.wsj.com/digits/2015/08/06/tencent-google-capital-invest-in-indian-healthcare-startup-practo/.
107. Ibid.
108. Paula Chakravartty and Yuezhi Zhao, "Toward a Transcultural Political Economy of Global Communication," in *Global Communication: Toward a Transcultural Political Economy*, eds. Paula Chakravartty and Yuezhi Zhao (Lanham, MD: Rowman & Littlefield, 2008), 11.
109. He Wei, "Ma Shares Thoughts on 'Digital China'," *China Daily*, March 6, 2018, accessed January 23, 2019, www.chinadaily.com.cn/a/201803/06/WS5a9df0c3a3106e7dcc13fc88.html.

4 Cultural Profile

Tencent, as an Internet giant, substantially controls a variety of online value-added services (VAS) in China's Internet industry, including IM, social networking, online entertainment, gaming, and e-commerce, among others. This chapter turns to the cultural sphere to review Tencent's popular products and cultural influences and their connection to its transnationalization strategies. After an overview of Tencent's cultural products, the chapter dives into the two most popular and successful products and services—mobile chat and digital gaming—and discusses how Tencent managed to monetize its mobile chat apps and VAS, including QQ and WeChat, through a bittersweet relation with China's major telecom carriers. Tencent's roadmap to becoming a global giant in the game industry used the gaming sector as an entry point to gain transnational competitiveness. Building upon its advantages in numbers of users, capital power, and global reach, Tencent has not only established itself as a vertically integrated global gaming empire—from engine services to game development and to publishing and distribution—but and also formed a cultural synergy of gaming, mobile and online communication, and social networking. The chapter concludes with an evaluation of Tencent's overall transnationalization strategies in the cultural industries.

Tencent's Cultural Products

Tencent's flagship products—QQ, WeChat, and online games—generate the greatest portion of revenues annually. They form a unique cultural brand for the company and a community for its diverse users.

QQ

As one of the first free instant messaging (IM) services in China, QQ accumulated registered users very quickly. In May 2000, within only half a year of its debut, OICQ's online users reached 100,000. "As a domestically developed online paging software, OICQ was the best. It brought us a lot of conveniences and friends," *People's Daily* commented on May 29, 2000.[1]

Table 4.1 Number of QQ Accounts, 2004–18

Year	*Account*	
	Registered User (Million)	*Active User (Million)*
2004	369.7	134.8
2005	492.6	201.9
2006	580.5	232.6
2007	741.7	300.2
2008	891.9	376.6
2009	*	522.9
2010		647.6
2011		721.0
2012		798.2
2013		808.0
2014		815.3
2015		853.1
2016		868.5
2017		783.4
2018		807.1

* Tencent no longer documented this item starting with the 2009 annual report.
Note: Figures are for the last 16 days of the fiscal year, ending December 31.

Sources: Tencent, Annual Reports, 2004–18 (revenue year-end of December 31).

The popularity did not bring much profit for Tencent at the beginning, though. Instead, to maintain the server, Tencent had to throw in a great deal of money, which caused its serious financial difficulties in 1999 and 2000.

It was not until QQ became available on mobile devices that Tencent was able to monetize it. Mobile QQ is similar to QQ in function, as mobile QQ allows users to exchange instant messages through preinstalled QQ software on mobile SIM cards and devices. In order to make this work, Tencent collaborated with telecommunication carriers and device manufacturers. When users chat with friends on their mobile phones via QQ and related services, they bring traffic and, hence, revenues to telecom operators' networks. A large portion, 63.6 percent, of Tencent's 2003 revenues in mobile and telecom VAS came from the mobile-data fees that mobile users paid with their subscriptions; the fee was determined by fixed terms with Chinese telecom giants.[2] Tencent also worked with mobile device manufacturers to "preload QQ client software on the advanced mobile phones and conduct joint marketing activities to customize the QQ client software for various mobile handset environments."[3]

Enterprise IM

In addition to personal services, Tencent also developed IM products for corporate communication. In April 2002, Tencent first launched BQQ, a corporate version of QQ for business communication within an enterprise.[4] In August 2003, Tencent upgraded BQQ and launched a new product, Real Time eXchange (RTX).[5] In working with individual companies, Tencent helped to build internal communication networks that allowed corporate employees to communicate instantly and locally.[6] In the following years, Tencent collaborated with IBM and Cisco in developing RTX, IBM and Cisco providing their expertise in enterprise communication services and software technologies.[7] Some important customers included Postal Savings Bank of China, Jiangsu Provincial Taxation Bureau, Air China Limited, the northwestern branch of Sinopec Group, and Chia Tai Group.[8]

Weixin and WeChat

On January 21, 2011, Tencent released a mobile device-based chatting service, Weixin and WeChat, with Weixin the name for its Chinese services and WeChat the one targeting overseas users.[9] The core service is based on instant messaging, but Weixin/WeChat is more than just a chatting tool. It integrates other value-added functions and eventually became a gateway for users to connect online and offline lives and to integrate the two in one app. Upon its launch, Weixin/WeChat gained immediate growth and has quickly become a major communications and social platform for smartphone users in China.[10]

Other VAS of social networking, entertainment, gaming, e-commerce, group purchases, local business reviews, online payments, and others were constantly added onto the Weixin and WeChat platform, which made it a multifunction hub for online lifestyles. For example, Weixin/WeChat Moments, a feature to share experiences, blogs, photos, and articles through publishing to users' Weixin/WeChat contacts, became another social platform for user interactions, in addition to Tencent's well-established QZone, the personal home page.[11] Weixin/WeChat Payment, to give another instance, an integrated online payment service, offers further monetization channels for Tencent through online advertising and e-commerce transactions:

> With the increasing popularity of Weixin Pay, bank handling fees related to C2C payment transactions via Weixin Pay, mainly arising from money transfers, increased significantly, amounting to over RMB 300 million (net of related revenue we received from users) for the month of January 2016.[12]

Table 4.2 Weixin and WeChat Combined Monthly Active Users (MAU) (Millions)

	2011	*2012*	*2013*	*2014*	*2015*	*2016*	*2017*	*2018*
Active users	–	160.8	355.0	500.0	697.0	889.3	988.6	1097.6

Sources: Tencent, Annual Reports, 2013–18 (revenue year-end of December 31).

QQ Game Portal

Tencent started out entertainment service with casual mini-games, such as "board games, card games and other games of skill" in 2003 through QQ Game Portal, a program bundled with the QQ software package.[13] Free to users and giving easy access to basic game services, QQ Game Portal quickly attracted a large number of users and became the largest casual-game portal in China.[14] New games, such as QQ Tang (a 2004 collection of a few mini-games for friends), QQ Speed (a self-developed car racing game), and QQ Dancer (a 2008 musical dancing game), were continually launched, and Tencent monetized them by adding fee-based subscriptions and game accessories for purchase.[15] In view of its growing popularity, Tencent launched Game Center on both Mobile QQ and Weixin/WeChat in 2013, which immediately contributed over $96.93 million (RMB 600 million) to the revenue in that year.[16]

Massive Multiplayer Online Games (MMOG)

Another real moneymaker for Tencent was its massive multiplayer online game (MMOG) business. Tencent, on the one hand, actively sought licenses from foreign game developers and imported games permitted under the Chinese regulations.[17] According to China's Ministry of Culture (MOC) regulations on online cultural activities, any party who wanted to operate imported online games in China needed to apply for MOC's approval of both the contents of and the license contracts for them.[18] Tencent brought the first MMOG into China in April 2003, which was *Sephiroth*, licensed by Korean developer Imazic.[19] *Dungeon and Fighter* (DNF)—a well-liked MMOG developed by Neople and Samsung—to give another example, was licensed to Tencent for its Chinese distribution in 2007 and launched in June 2008.[20] DNF gained peak concurrent users (PCU) of 1.2 million at the end of that year.

On the other hand, Tencent was also devoted to creating its own MMOG by primarily adopting Chinese storylines. In 2007 Tencent launched its first self-developed MMOG *QQ SanGuo*, which features the ancient Chinese history of the wars among three kingdoms around AD 220 to 280.[21] *QQ Huaxia*, another MMOG launched in the same year, was codeveloped by Tencent and Shenzhen Domain Computer Network Co. Ltd., a Tencent investee company.[22] This game was also plotted against the background of an ancient, mythical China.[23] More games of this style, such as *Silk Road Hero*, *Hero Island*, and *World of West*, were developed between 2009 and 2011.[24]

First-Person Shooting (FPS)

In addition to MMOG, Tencent made an effort in developing FPS genre in 2007 when it gained the licensing of *CrossFire* by Neowiz.[25] Launched in 2008, the game achieved one million PCU in 2009, which was a world record.[26] Carrying on the success, Tencent introduced another Korean-developed FPS game, *A.V.A.*, in 2010 by working with Neowiz again as its Chinese agent.[27]

Children's Games

In July 2010, Tencent entered the children's game segment by launching *Roco Kingdom*, which later became an online-gaming community for children from 7 to 14.[28] Adapting from the storyline in the game, Tencent later produced a series of animated movies that won a box office of $24.4 million (RMB 150 million).[29]

As Tencent's gaming kingdom grew large, the company started an international expansion through mergers and acquisitions. In 2010 it acquired a major stake of 92.78 percent in Riot Games and became the parent company of the U.S.-based online-game developer and publisher of *League of Legends*, a widely played game across the world.[30] In 2015 Riot Games became a wholly owned subsidiary of Tencent.[31] In June 2016 Tencent bought a majority stake in Supercell, a Finnish mobile-game developer and the publisher of *Clash of Clans*, for $8.6 billion.[32] The company's roadmap to becoming a global game giant is discussed further in the following sections.

Besides these superstars in chat platforms and games, in recent years, Tencent has put enormous efforts in the broadly defined cultural industry, including online publication and e-reading, online music and streaming services, and the previously discussed media and movie industry.

Online Publication and Reading Service

Tencent had only launched its own online reading service in 2014.[33] In early 2015 Tencent and Shanda formed China Reading Ltd., moving their own online publishing and literature services, namely, Tencent Literature and Shanda Cloudary, together into one company specializing in online publishing and e-book services.[34] Shanda Group, founded in Shanghai in 1999, was originally an online game company and became an investment group that focused on "financial services, technology and healthcare sectors."[35] The newly launched China Reading Ltd. was codirected by Tencent Literature's former CEO Wu Wenhui and Shanda Cloudary's former CEO Liang Xiaodong. Tencent held a majority 66.4 percent stake in China Reading.[36]

With Tencent being a latecomer, the deal, more like an acquisition than a merger, made China Reading the largest online publishing and e-book company in China.[37] Said to have more than 600 million registered users in China, China Reading in 2017 was planning an initial public offering in Hong Kong.[38]

Online Music

In July 2016 Tencent partnered with China Music Corp. in promoting the digital music business and acquired a majority stake of 61.6 percent of China Music Corp. The two joined Tencent's QQ Music and China Music Corporation's KuGou and Kuwo to form a new company, Tencent Music Entertainment Group, with Tencent's vice president Pang Kar Shun as CEO and China Music Corporation's co-CEOs Xie Guomin and Xie Zhenyu as copresidents.[39] The alliance created a dominant player in China's music-streaming market, as China Music Corp. KuGou and Kuwo each occupied 28 percent and 13 percent of the mobile music market, respectively, with another 15 percent owned by QQ Music.[40] In addition to a majority market share, the strategic merger was expected to advance the battle against online piracy in China, considering that the combined exclusive content licenses held by Tencent and China Music Corp. represented "more than 60 percent of all available music rights in China."[41]

In December 2017, Tencent started a collaboration with the Sweden-based music-streaming giant Spotify through a minority stake exchange, which would allow Spotify and Tencent's music subsidiary Tencent Music Entertainment (TME) to each hold a minority equity stake in the other.[42] In the following October, Tencent Music Entertainment (TME) filed an IPO prospectus, at which time Tencent owned 58.1% of TME's shares and Spotify owned 9.1 percent. TME became publicly traded at NYSE on December 12, 2018.[43]

From QQ to WeChat

For a closer look into the development of QQ and WeChat, next examined are the strategies to promote the QQ brand as a cultural synergy, followed by a discussion on the challenges Tencent encountered, especially with major Chinese telecom carriers.

Building a QQ Community

Taking advantage of QQ's popularity and user base, Tencent launched a set of fee-based VAS that construct an interactive online community. Users within this community, through purchasing different services, are able to individualize their virtual profiles, interact with friends or strangers, and play casual games, among other activities, all of which were centered around the QQ brand, such as Premium QQ, QQ Show, QQ Fantasy, QQ Pet, QQ Magic, QQ Ring, QQ Farm, and QQ Ranch, to name a few.[44] The QQ-related VAS have become a new time-space for self-display, self-expression, relationship maintenance and establishment, and entertainment.[45]

Tencent launched QQ Membership Club in November 2000, which was a higher-level IM service based on a monthly membership fee.[46] By paying a monthly charge of $1.20 (RMB 10.00), users were able to buy additional services to individualize their QQ usage, such as the ability to choose their own QQ numbers, store message logs on QQ servers, to have 100 megabytes storage space, free credits to use various QQ VAS (including online entertainment services), special signs indicating their QQ membership status, and exclusive access to additional chat rooms.[47] To take a QQ number as an example, when a user registers a free QQ account, the program would randomly assign the user a unique identification number. A member who pays a premium fee could choose a specific number, very often one that represented a date with special meaning, such as a birthday or anniversary. The service has gotten so popular that Tencent now has an entire website—haoma.com—to manage the selling and issuing of customized QQ numbers. Some parents would even buy a QQ number for their yet-to-be-born children as a gift based on the date and time of birth. Romantic partners would choose a QQ number that symbolizes their relationship.[48] In a way, QQ is no longer just a chat tool but is sold and exchanged as a commodity that represents the consumer's name and identity online.

The fee-based QQ membership later developed into a tier-based system that is integrated into every aspect of Tencent's value-added services. The system has nine tiers from "ordinary users" to "SVIP8," each level enjoying a different set of benefits and privileges.[49] For example, an ordinary user without paying any premium fee can have up to 500 QQ friends and 2G online storage. At SVIP8, the highest level, the user is able to have up to 2,000 QQ friends, two chatting groups of 2,000 people, storage of up to 1,400 personalized stickers on the account, a 500G online photo album, 2.5T online storage, and 350 QQ coins redeemable for other services within the QQ system.[50] All of these symbolize a privileged "social-economic status" in the QQ universe. Other similar privileges relate to gaming, shopping, and decoration in Tencent's online community.[51] Gaming privileges, for instance, include early access to newly released games and free toolkit packages for game use, promotions, and discounts, among others; shopping privileges connect online lifestyles to offline activities by providing users with offline shopping coupons; users could also customize their account skins, decorate homepages, and individualize profile avatars.[52]

To implement the premium membership system, a variety of micro-applications installed in QQ software let users customize their profile pictures and message-notification ringtones, play casual games, raise virtual pets, and so on. QQ Show, one of the earliest and most successful micro-apps, was a virtual avatar system that allowed users to choose an individual virtual character and pay for "virtual clothing, hairstyles, scenes and accessories" to decorate their profile images.[53] The service was carried out in

January 2003 and commercially run two months later.[54] Tencent promoted the service by first providing particular QQ Show items free. The company gradually introduced new features to the service with different levels of charges.[55]

Rivals in IM

As discussed in Chapter 2, the success of QQ was partly owed to Tencent's partnership with major Chinese telecom carriers who allowed mobile QQ to be preinstalled on their mobile SIM cards. At the same time when Tencent collaborated with China Mobile, China Unicom, and China Telecom, these giants to different extents felt the threat posed by Tencent's mobile QQ, which provided text messaging, voice communication, and visual exchanges, among other VAS, at a price lower than the common charges through traditional telecom channels.

These state-backed telecom titans first approached the problem by renegotiating terms in their partnerships with Tencent. In October 2004, as former Tencent executive Chengmin Liu related, China Mobile called for a sudden meeting with Tencent and asked to redefine the rates collected out of one MVAS—the 161 Mobile Chat.[56] According to Liu, the 161 Mobile Chat represented a significant portion of Tencent's overall earnings, which left Tencent little bargaining power with China Mobile.[57] On December 22, 2004, Tencent announced in an official release that it was in negotiations with China Mobile on the matter.[58] In view of the fact that 161 Mobile Chat contributed 10 percent and 16 percent of Tencent's net profit in the calendar year 2003 and the half year ended June 30, 2004, respectively, Tencent's monthly net profit from 161 Mobile Chat would be reduced by approximately $484,000 (RMB 4 million) with China Mobile's new terms.[59] In January 2005, the two companies terminated their shared fee-collection agreements, and Tencent only received "a predetermined monthly maintenance fee" until the end of June 2005.[60]

As a result, revenues immediately declined in Tencent's mobile and telecommunication sectors: "Revenues from our mobile and telecommunications value-added services decreased by 19.3 percent to RMB 517.3 million for the year ended 31 December 2005 from RMB 641.2 million for the year ended 31 December 2004."[61]

A collateral damage was the unprecedented drop of Tencent's stock price, which fell by over 8 percent during negotiations with China Mobile in December 2004.[62] During the next two years, Tencent engaged in an array of buyback and repurchase of its own shares.[63] Analysts said that this was aimed to show the company's confidence in its continual growth.[64]

A second move, taken by telecom carriers, was to start their own instant-messaging products. As early as 2003, China Telecom started developing

Vnet Messenger (VIM), a service to connect landline phones, lower-end cell phones (Little Smart), and mobile phones for chatting, document transmission, and video chatting.[65] Little Smart ran on a much-cheaper technology than GSM or CDMA and "used wireless local loop (WILL) technology to connect mobile devices with traditional landline networks, with its own set of base stations, switchers, and handsets."[66] Bound with China Telecom's broadband services, VIM was also an integral platform for entertainment VAS, such as browsing pictures and downloading ringtones and mobile games for household desktops. "It was a reasonable move for China Telecom to develop its own IM," according to one VIM R&D staff member, commenting on the growing threats that traditional phone services were faced with.[67] Not enough data suggests whether VIM was a successful move or not. Upon its acquisition of China Unicom's CDMA business in 2008, China Telecom, with the 3G licenses granted by the state, launched a new mobile and desktop IM app—e-Surfing live—that integrated instant information services with voice and data communication.[68]

China Telecom was not alone. In 2006 and 2007, China Mobile and China Unicom both developed their own instant-messaging systems. China Mobile launched a mobile-to-PC IM service, Fetion. Initially, an IM platform only for China Mobile's cell-phone subscribers who were able to exchange messages between computers and cell phones, Fetion enjoyed a dramatic growth during Tencent's fight with Qihoo 360 and eventually opened up to all mobile users, including those of China Unicom and China Telecom in November 2010.[69] China Unicom, on the other side, launched a mobile-Internet instant-messaging app, Chaoxin, in 2007, which was later shut down in 2009 when its CDMA business was relocated to China Telecom.[70]

At the end of 2006, Tencent and China Mobile revisited their terms of collaborations on Mobile QQ. Prior to this, China Mobile was said to have terminated collaborations with all major IM service providers, including Tencent, in order to promote its own IM application.[71] The negotiation resulted in a "cooperation memorandum" to jointly develop the two companies' IM platforms and to extend their contracts for another half a year, during which they would together launch Fetion QQ.[72] According to the plan, Fetion QQ would realize the "interconnection between China Mobile's Fetion handset users and QQ subscribers."[73]

Debate on Weixin/WeChat

The coexistence of QQ, Fetion, and other mobile messaging apps remained for several years until January 2011, when Tencent launched its mobile social application Weixin/WeChat as an integral site for free text and multimedia messages, video calls, photo sharing, mobile games, e-commerce, and e-life, among others.[74] Telecom carriers' SMS took an immediate hit, as Weixin/WeChat provided convenient text-message service at a much lower price than SMS. Traditionally, SMS was charged according to the number of messages sent. One message, regardless of length, was $0.01 (RMB 0.1). The cost of Weixin/WeChat, however, was based on the amount of the data traffic through general packet radio service (GPRS). For every 1 MB of data streamed via GPRS, users could send thousands of text messages by Weixin/WeChat and only be charged a total of $0.15 (RMB 1.00).[75] Weixin/WeChat, quickly diffused among QQ users, is said to have taken away 20 percent of the SMS businesses immediately, which totaled half a year's profits for China Unicom and China Telecom combined in 2011.[76] Taking the hit hard, China Unicom and China Mobile launched their own Weixin-like mobile applications in 2011, WO and Feiliao, respectively. Neither turned out to be a noticeable counterweight to Tencent's Weixin/WeChat. In July 2013 China Mobile aborted its Feiliao business, while China Unicom chose to work with Tencent in promoting the customized SIM card for packaged deals of Weixin/WeChat services.[77]

The challenge posed by over-the-top content (OTT) providers to traditional telecom carriers did not stand out as a unique phenomenon in China. It was a natural trend because the growing Internet industry would want to expand both horizontally and vertically and to enlarge business territory. It was essentially a battle between the different units of capital for the limited resources possessed by users. Dong-Hee Shin analyzed the rise of mobile voice over Internet protocol (mVoIP) in Korea that had resulted in a decline in voice calls carried by mobile operators.[78] In the European and North American contexts, the growing popularity of social media, such as Facebook and Twitter, and online-streaming platforms, such as Netflix, Hulu, and YouTube, brought similar challenges to telecom and cable operators.[79] How the Internet firms and telecom operators negotiated the terms, however, varied depending on the specific context. For Tencent, the triumph of Weixin/WeChat came as a negotiated outcome among the telecom carriers, the Internet companies, and China's central regulatory entities.

First, the rise of Weixin/WeChat fell along the national strategy to converge three networks—telecommunications, broadcasting and TV network, and the Internet. In January 2010 in a State Council meeting, Premier Wen Jiabao pushed for the integration of the three networks.[80] This was not just about reconsolidating national infrastructural networks but an important strategy to further open up domestic communication markets to additional players who were traditionally kept from service provision or content production, such as equipment manufacturer or Internet VAS providers.

The central government made another gesture when in 2014 the National Development and Reform Commission (NDRC) and Ministry of Industry and Information Technology (MIIT) jointly announced a notice to liberalize pricing of the telecommunications services.[81] The message was clear: to further open up the domestic telecom industry, to encourage and protect domestic Internet capital, and to rebalance the national political economy by accelerating the "Chinese-style digital capitalism."[82]

It was under this context that MIIT played a critical role in protecting Tencent's advantage with Weixin/WeChat. In early 2013, there was a heated debate over whether telecom carriers should charge additional fees either on Tencent or users for using Weixin/WeChat, considering how much impact Weixin/WeChat had on the carriers' SMS services. According to a statistic announced by the MIIT in March 2013, the growth rates of SMS business and telephone business in the first two months of 2013 were much lower than those of the mobile Internet businesses.[83] Telecom carriers insisted that there should be additional charges to Tencent for maintaining the network infrastructure because Tencent services took so much advantage of it.[84] In February and March 2013, MIIT called for multiple meetings of telecom operators and Tencent to coordinate their requests. MIIT's attitude, however, was ambiguous and inexplicit. On the one hand, MIIT head Miao Wei acknowledged the validity of telecom carriers' concerns, as they had to expend money and effort in managing the network. On the other hand, Miao also noted that this problem should be solved by a competitive market mechanism, the principle of which was to contain telecom giants' monopoly power and to encourage the growth of innovative Internet companies. More of mediation than regulation, MIIT asked China Mobile, China Telecom, and China Unicom not to collude on this matter, and they were instructed to negotiate terms with Tencent separately.[85]

Under the guideline to "follow the market rule," MIIT instructed that China Mobile, China Telecom, and China Unicom were not supposed to form an alliance in negotiating with Tencent. Previous telecom history already suggests an enduring rivalry among the three, not to mention their different approaches in responding to the Weixin/WeChat challenge. China Telecom started working with Tencent by launching QQ service on its CDMA mobile devices in as early as 2011.[86] Any China Telecom user can use his or her phone number as the QQ numbers to log onto Mobile QQ, along with other services on the mobile phones certified by China Telecom.[87] In terms of Weixin/WeChat, China Telecom suggested that it was an opportunity, instead of conflict, for further collaboration in its data business. The president of China Unicom also implied that the relationship with Tencent should be an interdependent one rather than a water-fire antagonism.[88] Both China Telecom and China Unicom shortly launched their own versions of contract cell phones with preinstalled Weixin/WeChat. China Mobile, for the moment, was sticking to its own Fetion service.

Game Industry as Game Changer

In a different theater, Tencent used the game sector as an entry point to gain transnational competitiveness. Building upon its advantage in its user base, capital power, and global reach, Tencent was vertically integrated as a global game empire from engine service through game development to production and distribution.

The Chinese Distributor and Operator

Tencent states in its prospectus, "Online games currently are one of the fastest growing online services in China. We develop and source online games for our customers."[89] Collaborating with foreign game developers and publishers, mostly Korea- and U.S.-based, provided a convenient path for Tencent, especially at the company's infant stage when it was not competitive enough to offer appealing game contents and services. Tencent started representing foreign-developed games as their Chinese distributor and operator in 2003 when it first worked with Korean game company Imazic for the distribution of a massive multiplayer online game (MMOG)—*Sephiroth*. *Sephiroth*, the Chinese name of which is *QQ Kaixuan*, was Tencent's first MMOG for commercial operation.[90] Although a popular one, the game was shut down in 2009 due to the termination of license from Imazic.[91]

Many of Tencent's popular games in varying genres were launched through such an importing-distributing-operating strategy, including Korean game publisher Neowiz's online music-related rollerblade racing game: *R2Beat*; German game developer Crytek's first-person-shooter game *Warface*; Korea-based Webzen's *Battery*; Korean company Vertigo Games' *War of the Zombie*; Korean developer Nextplay's popular MMOG *Punch Monster*; San Francisco-based social-game developer Zynga's localized *Cityville* on QZone, among others.[92]

These collaborations formed a symbiosis between Tencent and foreign game developers. The relationship proved beneficial. For overseas game developers, by taking advantage of Tencent's local user base, they often found their games to be well accepted in China. For Tencent, securing exclusive licenses of popular online and mobile games from foreign developers and publishers not only attracted more Chinese players to Tencent's network but also made it convenient to promote Tencent's own games.[93] A seemingly win-win strategy helped to sustain Tencent's dominance in China's gaming market, as well as to tighten Tencent's relation with foreign developers for further collaborations.

Vertical Integration Through Investments

A second and more important strategy that Tencent took—when it had grown bigger—was to acquire minority or majority stakes in other players in the global PC, console, and mobile gaming markets.[94] The first move of this kind was in 2006 when Tencent bought 16.9 percent of the equity interest in GoPets Ltd., a Korean corporation that developed and published interactive games, such as raising virtual pets.[95] Between 2008 and 2010, Tencent invested in a few online and mobile-game developers, though the details of the deals are scant. Among them, Tencent gained 20.02 percent of equity interest in a "Southeast Asia-based online game company" in 2008 and raised its stake to 30.02 percent as of the end of 2009.[96] In 2010 alone, Tencent acquired equity interests in seven online-game development firms based in Southeast Asia, East Asia, or the United States, based with varying stakes from 10 percent to 49 percent.[97]

Whereas these unspecified deals involved small expenditures, Tencent launched some large-scale mergers and acquisitions beginning in 2011. These displayed distinctive characteristics of vertical integration in the gaming industry.

In 2012 and 2013 Tencent purchased enough equity to ultimately own 67 percent of Level Up, the online game and game-magazine publisher, mentioned in Chapter 3, that primarily operated in the Philippines, India, Brazil, and some other parts of Latin America.[98] The deal helped Tencent "identify further opportunities in" the emerging markets of Brazil and the Philippines.[99] Tencent's game distributing businesses, since 2012, further extended into Activision Blizzard's territory. Activision Blizzard, "the world's most profitable pure-play game publisher and a global leader in interactive entertainment," set foot in China by collaborating with Tencent for its blockbuster franchise *Call of Duty*.[100] In addition to an exclusive license to operate *Call of Duty* in Mainland China, Tencent also subscribed a 6 percent partnership interest in Activision Blizzard with about $429 million (RMB 2.638 billion).[101] While Tencent's effort to explore distribution rights for various games was ongoing, in 2017 Tencent achieved another landmark victory when it won the right to publish that year's blockbuster online multiplayer battle royale game *PlayerUnknown's Battlegrounds* (PUBG) in China on mobile and smart platforms.[102]

Then Tencent moved upstream in the business chain by entering the game-engine market, which would provide the technical and, especially, software support for game visualization in various genres and settings.[103] This was primarily achieved through Tencent's investment in the U.S.-incorporated Epic Games. In July 2012 Tencent acquired 48.4 percent of equity shares in Epic Games, which specializes in 3D game-engine technology and had reputable collaborations with Electronic Arts (EA).[104]

Even greater efforts were put in expanding into the game-development sector—a main battlefield in the industry—both in online and mobile businesses. Riot Games, a U.S.-based developer and publisher of the well-known massive online battle arena (MOBA) game *League of Legends*, which boasted more than 100 million monthly active players as of

September 2016, became a wholly owned subsidiary of Tencent as of the end of 2015.[105] The acquisition was achieved through a series of arrangements initiated since 2008. In November 2008 the two companies entered into a licensing partnership that gave Tencent the exclusive license to distribute Riot Games' under-development title *League of Legends: Clash of Fates*.[106] In February 2011 Tencent strengthened its links to the widely distributed game by acquiring a majority interest of 92.78 percent in Riot Games, prior to which Tencent held a minority of 22.34 percent.[107] Subsequent to the deal, Tencent was set for the beta opening of *League of Legends* in China while Riot Games remained independent in its own operations and management.[108] In 2015 Tencent acquired the remaining shares of Riot Games and became its parent company.[109]

In 2015 Tencent further expanded in the U.S. market by acquiring 14.6 percent stake in Glu Mobile, a San Francisco-based mobile-game developer.[110] The deal was closed at an 11 percent premium to Glu's closing price at the time, as Tencent paid $126 million for 21 million shares.[111] As a result of the partnership, Steven Ma, Tencent's senior vice president for the interactive entertainment division, joined Glu's board of directors in April 2015. Although Glu Mobile was famous for its mobile games associated with celebrities, such as *Kim Kardashian: Hollywood* and *Gordon Ramsay: DASH*, the collaboration was aimed at bringing Tencent's Weixin/WeChat-based smartphone shooter game—WeFire—to overseas markets, including North and South America, Europe, the Middle East, Africa, Australia, New Zealand, and others.[112]

In the Asian market, through a range of agreements in 2014, Tencent bought around 28 percent interest in a Korean online and mobile-game developer and publisher, Netmarble Games Corp., better known by its former name CJ Games Corp.[113]

At the same time, integration into the mobile-gaming sector was consolidated when a high-profile trade—its buy-in in Supercell, the developer of the hit game *Clash of Clans*—took place in mid-2016.[114] With a record-breaking price of $8.6 billion, Tencent bought the Finland-based company from SoftBank, the Japanese telecommunications and Internet corporation that was an important institutional shareholder of the Chinese e-commerce giant Alibaba.[115] While Supercell strengthened Tencent's arm in mobile gaming with the popular and fast-growing *Clash of Clans*, the strategic partnership also gave Supercell access to "hundreds of millions of new gamers via Tencent's channels" in China.[116]

As a unique arena of global and local cultural interactions, the digital gaming industry has become a potentially strategic market in transnational capitalism. Tencent, through a carefully unfolding and integrating process, was able to position itself as an important force transnationally in the game industry, more than in other submarkets of the Internet industry, such as IM or social media. The game sector, in this sense, was prospectively a critical "game changer" in Tencent's reach for global power.

Transnationalizing the Tencent Brand

Tencent's growth in QQ, WeChat, and the game industry showed a clear path to extend its influences from domestic to global markets. As Tencent started incorporating transnational elements into its capital structure at an early stage—two years after the company's birth, the company was active in making overseas investments. According to the company's reports in past years, it had investments, aside from Mainland China and Hong Kong, in North America, Asia, Europe, and other parts of the world. The company rearranged the ways to present overseas investments by regions a few times. Table 4.3 shows Tencent's overseas investments in four sections, which

Table 4.3 Tencent's Yearly Investments by Region, 2004–18 (RMB Million)

Early Years					
Year	*Hong Kong*	*United States*	*Europe*	*Other Countries*	
2004	589.831	542.598	519.874	174.437	
2005	282.157	862.921	376.891	83.255	
2006	231.386	566.695	301.549	74.561	
2007	550.911	735.705	630.795	10.044	
Beginning of Shift					
Year	*Mainland China*	*Hong Kong*	*United States*	*Europe*	*Other Asian Countries*
2008	2.055	819.670	106.240	400.559	329.398
2009	90.244	564.321	49.949	341.410	644.784
2010	446.608	2,735	159.719	3,869	886.024
Focus on Korea in Other Regions					
Year	*Mainland China*	*Hong Kong*	*United States*	*Europe*	*Other Regions*
2011	4,410	3,538	206.962	2,658	1,145
2012	4,818	6,382	2,938	3,974	2,435
2013	10,726	10,535	4,185	6,235	3,478
2014	43,106	17,804	6,066	3,327	14,849
Reorganization and Expansion in North America					
Year	*Mainland China and Hong Kong*	*North America*	*Europe*	*Asia Excluding Mainland China and Hong Kong*	*Others*
2015	85,282	14,412	2, 462	9, 036	93
2016	108,715	22,310	21,645	11,322	113
2017	161,903	52,542	34,515	26,407	250
2018	254,992	44,835	37,451	30,148	1760

Sources: Tencent, Annual Reports, 2004–18.

reveal the way the company organized its foreign businesses and reflect shifts in Tencent's business focus throughout the years.

As revealed by the company's financial reports since 2004, early years' investments, between 2004 and 2007, were primarily in financial instruments, such as "held-to-maturity investments, trading investments, term deposits and cash and cash equivalents."[117] By comparing volumes to those in later years, the early years' financial investments were not as significant as the business deals Tencent later made. In 2008 investments in associates and, particularly, in Southeast Asian countries begin to stand out as a major focus.

Korea was the focus for 2013 and 2014. Of the $562 million (RMB 3.5 billion) invested in other regions in 2013, $279 million (RMB 1.8 billion) went into Korea. In 2014, of the $2.4 billion (RMB 14.8 billion) invested in other regions, $1.1 billion (RMB 6.4 billion) went to Korea.

In recent years, investments expanded to both financial and nonfinancial forms, such as associates, redeemable preference shares of associates, joint ventures, and available-for-sale financial assets.[118] In 2015 Tencent reorganized its spreadsheet again by putting Mainland China and Hong Kong together, enlarging the United States into the North American region, and adding another section on other Asian areas excluding Mainland China and Hong Kong.

On the revenue side, as of 2018, the revenue from overseas markets was $1.35 billion (RMB 9.037 billion), accounting for 2.9 percent of Tencent's total revenues.

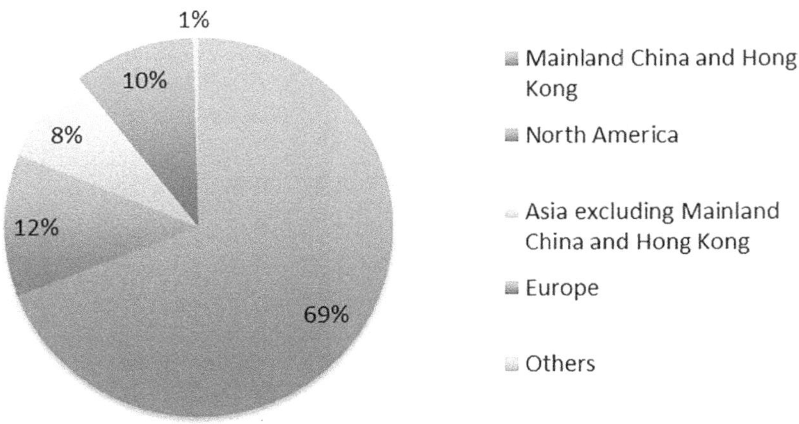

Figure 4.1 Tencent's Investments by Regions in 2018

Source: Tencent, Annual Report, 2018.

Table 4.4 Tencent's Yearly Revenues Outside China, 2009–18

Year	*Revenue (RMB Million)*	*Percentage of Total Revenue*
2009	5.649	0.05
2010	13.914	0.07
2011	468.556	1.6
2012	2,158.610	4.9
2013	4,459	7.4
2014	6,470	8.2
2015	6,612	6.4
2016	7,566	4.9
2017	7,993	3.4
2018	9,037	2.89

Sources: Tencent, Annual Reports, 2009–18.

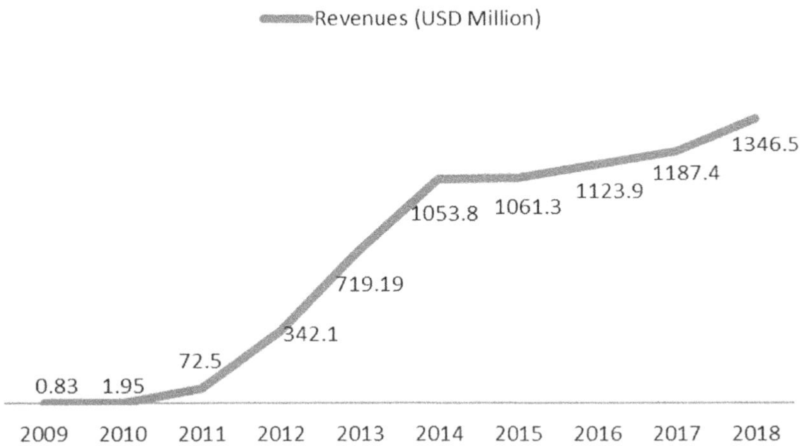

Figure 4.2 Tencent's Yearly Revenues Outside China, 2009–18

Sources: Tencent, Annual Reports, 2009–18.

Transnational activities took a variety of forms: market expansion of Tencent's services, investments in or acquisitions of foreign-based media and digital companies by purchasing stakes in them, research and development collaboration in working on data centers and network systems, strategic partnerships with foreign-based companies in jointly developing services, and strategic memoranda with giants from different media industries, among others.

Market expansion was primarily through the use of Tencent's IM services and value-added services of QQ, micro-blogging, QZone, and WeChat.

Tencent achieved this in several ways. First, it launched its services in multiple foreign languages. In December 2010 Tencent launched the first international version of QQ in English, Japanese, and French.[119] In 2011 Tencent launched the English service for its microblogging site.[120] For WeChat, the service in 2012 was available in two South Asia countries—India and Thailand.[121] As of 2018, WeChat was offered in 18 languages, including English, Indonesian, Spanish, Portuguese, Thai, Vietnamese, and Russian, and had over 70 million registered overseas users. In particular, WeChat enjoyed high popularity in South and Southeast Asian countries, such as India, Thailand, and Malaysia.[122]

Secondly, Tencent collaborated with local media companies and Internet service providers to both promote publicities and diffuse its products. In Indonesia, Tencent partnered with Indonesia PT Global Mediacom to launch a TV commercial campaign for WeChat in 2013.[123] The company even recruited soccer stars Lionel Messi of Argentina and Neymar da Silva Santos Júnior (Neymar) from Brazil for WeChat commercials.[124] Such an approach was made loud and clear when Ma Huateng revealed his plan to expand WeChat services and localized it by adapting it to Western users: "[The next step] will be to cooperate with local developers, for example with game developers to promote products, and also to adjust to Western user habits."[125] In late 2015 WeChat took another step further when its online payment service started fully opening to overseas purchases so that users could pay with RMB using WeChat, and the vendors would receive local currency for the transactions.[126]

In addition to the instant-messaging and social-media businesses, many investments, acquisitions, and strategic partnerships focused on games, unsurprisingly, with developers primarily based in South Korea and the West Coast of the United States. Tencent's intensive efforts put forward in the global game industry did not fully kick off until 2008, when it first invested $11 million in the San Francisco-based online-game company Outspark, together with two other investment partners, DCM and Altos Ventures.[127] Some major investments, as disclosed previously, include alliances with Zynga, Riot Games, Epic Games, Activision Blizzard, Netmarble Games, and Supercell, among others.

Last but not least, strategic partnerships with foreign media-content providers suggest a clear ambition of Tencent to enter cultural industry and, specifically, content production.[128] The first step the company took was to become an exclusive partner with U.S.-based TV, film, and music corporations and provide paid online-streaming services of their contents to Chinese users. Between 2013 and 2016, Tencent secured exclusive distribution licenses from Warner Bros. Pictures, Warner Music, Universal Studios, Miramax Films, Lionsgate, Pixar Studios, Marvel Studios, Sony Music Entertainment, HBO, Paramount, MGM, Walt Disney, 20th Century Fox, and ESPN's NBA, NCAA

Men's Basketball Championship Tournament, and the X Games.[129] These partnerships altogether built up Tencent's online-streaming kingdom as a unique content provider and distributor of the major Hollywood productions.

Conclusion

Tencent's cultural profile further exemplifies its strategy of integration and transnationalization. The brand's star products in instant messaging and chatting, including QQ, Weixin, and WeChat, have together successfully built an online community and cultural identity for Chinese users. While its mobile chat is primarily grounded on a popular domestic base, Tencent's establishment in the gaming industry has taken full advantage of its global collaborators as their distributors, operators, codevelopers, and/or investors.

The company's overall transnational expansion has unfolded gradually since its public offering in 2004 and featured a full-scale strategy that incorporated various forms of inter-capital relations, such as mergers and acquisitions, strategic alliances, service expansions, and research and development. With IM and gaming being two primary vectors, Tencent's IM and social-media services are predominantly expanded into South and Southeast Asia, while the collaborations and investments in the gaming sector are connected more closely with the capital units from the United States and Korea. Recent moves into media and cultural markets suggest a further diversification of Tencent's businesses.

Notes

1. "OICQ Users Reached 100, 000," *People's Daily*, May 29, 2000, accessed August 10, 2016, www.people.com.cn/GB/channel5/28/20000529/80561.html.
2. Ibid; Tencent, Annual Report, 2004, 6.
3. Ibid.
4. Wen, "Tengxun BQQ xiandai bangong xin liangdian" 腾讯BQQ现代办公新亮点 [Tencent's BQQ Brought New Highlight to Modern Office], *Zhonggong Jisuanji Bao 中国计算机报*, April 22, 2002.
5. Ying Hu, "Cong QQ2003 dao RTX" 从QQ2003到RTX [From QQ2003 to RTX], *Jisuanji Shijie 计算机世界*, August 25, 2003, E06.
6. Tencent, Prospectus, 92.
7. "Tencent Reached an Agreement with IBM for Close Cooperation in the Future," press release, *Tencent*, November 3, 2003, accessed March 20, 2017, www.tencent.com/en-us/articles/80237.html; "Cisco and Tencent Launch Unified Communications Solution for Chinese Market," press release, *Cisco*, September 9, 2010, accessed March 20, 2017, https://newsroom.cisco.com/press-release-content?type=webcontent&articleId=5692711.
8. RTX, "Successful Cases," *Tencent*, accessed March 20, 2017, http://rtx.tencent.com/rtx/case/index.shtml.
9. Jiulong Cheng, "Weixin PK duanxin Tengxun tiaodou yunying shang" 微信PK短信 腾讯挑逗运营商 [Weixin Versus Text Message Tencent Challenging Carriers], *21st Century Business Herald*, January 25, 2011, 20.

10. Tencent, Annual Report, 2012, 7.
11. Ibid.
12. Tencent, Annual Report, 2015, 7.
13. Tencent, Prospectus, 89.
14. Tencent, Annual Report, 2010, 10.
15. Ibid., Annual Report, 2004, 17; 2007, 8; 2008, 8; 2004, 17.
16. Ibid., Annual Report, 2013, 9.
17. Tencent, Prospectus, 42.
18. Ibid.
19. Le Wang, "Tengxun qianyue Imagic gongsi Sephiroth jinru zhongguo" 腾讯签约Imagic公司 Sephiroth进入中国 [Tencent Signed Contract with Imagic and Sephiroth Entered Chinese Market], *ChinaByte*, April 24, 2003, accessed August 20, 2016, http://news.chinabyte.com/371/1665371.shtml.
20. Tencent Annual Report, 2007, 8; 2008, 8.
21. Ibid., 8; "Games: QQ Sanguo Background," *Tencent*, accessed August 20, 2016, http://sg.qq.com/web2009/gamedata/gamedata_newpalyer.htm.
22. Tencent, Annual Report, 2007, 8.
23. "Interactive Entertainment Service," *Tencent*, accessed August 20, 2016, www.tencent.com/en-us/ps/ieservice.shtml.
24. Tencent, Annual Report, 2009, 8; 2010, 11.
25. Ibid.
26. Ibid., Annual Report, 2009, 8.
27. Ibid.
28. Ibid., Annual Report, 2010, 10.
29. Yue Wang, "Tencent Is Now Building a Movie Empire," *Forbes Asia*, September 17, 2014, accessed August 20, 2016, www.forbes.com/sites/ywang/2014/09/17/tencent-is-now-building-a-movie-empire/#139fdd7c6dc0.
30. Tencent, Annual Report, 2010, 190.
31. Ibid., Annual Report, 2015, 191.
32. Paul Carsten, Jussi Rosendahl, and Ritsuko Ando, "China's Tencent Buys 'Clash of Clans' Maker Supercell for $8.6 Billion," *Reuters*, accessed August 20, 2016, www.reuters.com/article/us-supercell-m-a-tencent-holdings-idUSKCN0Z716E.
33. Wu Nan, "China's Amazon? Tencent and Shanda to Merge Online Publishing and eBook Services," *South China Morning Post*, March 17, 2015, accessed September 5, 2016, www.scmp.com/lifestyle/technology/article/1740029/merger-chinese-online-publishing-sites-will-create-chinas.
34. Ibid.
35. "About Us," *Shanda*, accessed February 13, 2017, www.shanda.com/about-us.
36. Tencent, Annual Report, 2015, 191.
37. Ibid.
38. Zen Soo, "Tencent-Backed China Reading Plans IPO of Up to US$800 Million in Hong Kong, *South China Morning Post*, February 6, 2017, accessed February 16, 2017, www.techinasia.com/wechats-growing-empire-tencent-invested-acquired-2014.
39. Tencent, Interim Report, 2016, 66; "Financial Releases of 2016: China Music Corporation and Tencent's QQ Music Announce a Strategic Merger to Jointly Develop Digital Music Business in China," *Tencent*, July 15, 2016, accessed September 5, 2016, www.tencent.com/en-us/news_timeline.html.
40. Alec MacFarlane and Juro Osawa, "Tencent to Buy Majority Stake in China Music Corp., Creating Streaming Giant," *Wall Street Journal*, July 14, 2016, accessed September 5, 2016, www.wsj.com/articles/tencent-to-buy-majority-stake-in-china-music-corp-creating-streaming-giant-1468470851.
41. Ibid. "Financial Releases of 2016."

42. "Spotify, Tencent and Tencent Music Entertainment Announce Equity Investments," *Tencent*, December 8, 2017, accessed March 24, 2019, www.tencent.com/en-us/articles/16000721512809778.pdf.
43. Tencent Music Entertainment Group, "Form F-1 Registration Statement" (Prospectus), October 2, 2018, accessed March 24, 2019, www.sec.gov/Archives/edgar/data/1744676/000119312518290581/d624633df1.htm.
44. "Internet Value-Added Services," *Tencent*, accessed August 20, 2016, www.tencent.com/en-us/ps/internetservice.shtml.
45. Sonia Livingstone, "Taking Risky Opportunities in Youthful Content Creation: Teenagers' Use of Social Networking Sites for Intimacy, Privacy, and Self-Expression," *New Media & Society* 10, no. 3 (2008): 393–411; Dal Yong Jin, "Critical Analysis of User Commodities as Free Labour in Social Networking Sites: A Case Study of Cyworld," *Continuum* 29, no. 6 (2015): 938–50.
46. Lin and Zhang, *Ma Huateng de Tengxun Diguo*, 133.
47. Tencent, Prospectus, 87.
48. Ibid.
49. "Tier-Based Privileges," *QQ Membership*, accessed December 14, 2016, http://vip.qq.com/freedom./freedom_grade.html?ADTAG=www.tencent.com/en-us/ps/internetservice.shtml&SNO=1481753754605.
50. Ibid.
51. "Four Reasons to Join the Membership," *QQ Membership*, accessed December 14, 2016, http://vip.qq.com/help/why.html?ADTAG=www.google.com/&SNO=1481754886316.
52. Ibid.
53. "Internet Value-Added Services."
54. X. Wu, *Biography of Tencent*, 84–87.
55. Tencent, Prospectus, 89.
56. X. Wu, *Biography of Tencent*, 118.
57. Ibid.
58. "Tencent in Negotiation with China Mobile on '161 Mobile Chat' Agreement with China Mobile," 2004 Financial Releases, *Tencent*, December 24, 2004, accessed February 13, 2017, www.tencent.com/en-us/news_timeline.html.
59. Ibid. The currency exchange rate is based on "Historic United States Dollar Chinese Yuan Renminbi," accessed February 13, 2017, http://currencies.zone/historic/us-dollar/chinese-yuan/p68.
60. "Tencent Signs New '161 Mobile Chat' Agreement with China Mobile," 2004 Financial Releases, *Tencent*, January 18, 2005, accessed February 13, 2017, www.tencent.com/en-us/news_timeline.html.
61. Tencent, Annual Report, 2005, 16.
62. Sidney Luk, "Tencent Sees Lower Profit on China Mobile Deal," *South China Morning Post*, December 23, 2004.
63. "General Mandates to Issue and Repurchase Shares," *Tencent*, March 30, 2005, www.tencent.com/en-us/notice_timeline.html; "Voting Results at the 2005 Annual General Meeting of Tencent Holdings Limited," *Tencent*, April 27, 2005, www.tencent.com/en-us/notice_timeline.html.
64. "Tencent Announces 2005 Fourth Quarter and Annual Results," Financial Releases, *Tencent*, March 22, 2006, accessed September 8, 2016, www.tencent.com/en-us/news_timeline.html.
65. Xiaowu Cao, "Zhongguo Dianxin mizao VIM" 中国电信密造"VIM" 欲"拦截"虚拟运营商 [China Telecom Developed VIM], *21st Century Business Herald 21世纪经济报道*, November 22, 2003, accessed September 8, 2016, http://tech.sina.com.cn/it/t/2003-11-22/1636259281.shtml.

66. Qiu, *Working-Class Network Society*, 60.
67. Xiaowu Cao, "Sanda yunying sharu jishi tongxin Tengxun simian chuge" 三大运营杀入即时通信腾讯四面楚歌 [The Telecom Carriers Entered the IM Market], *21st Century Business Herald 21世纪经济报道*, December 18, 2003, accessed February 8, 2016, China Knowledge Resource Integrated Database (CNKI).
68. "E-surfing," *China Telecom*, accessed September 8, 2016, http://en.chinatelecom.com.cn/products/t20090227_48412.html; "Business Review 2009," *China Telecom*, accessed September 8, 2016, www.chinatelecom-h.com/en/ir/report/annual2009/online/Eng/bus_rev.html.
69. "3Q dazhan zhi feixin xiazai sousuo liang shangzhang 600%" 3Q大战"致飞信下载搜索量上涨600% [Fetion Received 600% More Download and Search Rates by Users Due to the 3Q War], *Saidi Wang 赛迪网*, November 4, 2010, accessed September 8, 2016, http://tech.ifeng.com/telecom/detail_2010_11/04/3006046_0.shtml; Chaoli Jin, "Feixin xuanbu xiang liantong dianxin yonghu kaifang" 飞信宣布向联通电信用户开放 [Fetion Now Open to Users of China Unicom and China Telecom], *Beijing Shangbao 北京商报*, November 8, 2010, accessed September 8, 2016, www.c114.net/topic/2428/a557142.html.
70. Xiaoyu Gu, "Zhongguo Dianxin jiang guanting yuanshu Zhongguo Liantong chaoxin ji UNIJA yewu" 中国电信将关停原属中国联通超信及UNIJA业务 [China Telecom to Shut Down the Chaoxin App Developed by China Unicom], *Jinghua Shibao 京华时报*, June 27, 2009, accessed September 8, 2016, http://tech.qq.com/a/20090627/000017.htm.
71. Yuanwei Xin, "mianlin duanliang daxian Tengxun wunai jiang tui mianfei Shouji QQ面临"断粮"大限 腾讯无奈将推免费"手机QQ" [Tencent May Have to Provide Mobile QQ for Free], *Jinghua Shibao 京华时报*, December 26, 2006, accessed February 13, 2017, http://news.xinhuanet.com/fortune/2006-12/26/content_5532052.htm.
72. Tencent, Annual Report, 2006, 7.
73. Ibid., 13.
74. "Weixin and WeChat," *Tencent*, accessed September 8, 2016, www.tencent.com/en-us/system.html.
75. Cheng, *Weixin PK duanxin*, 20.
76. Chunchao Wang, "Tengxun tui xin kehuduan gangshang feixin" 腾讯推新客户端杠上飞信 分流运营商超 600 亿短信收入 [Tencent to Launch New Service Challenging Fetion], *Tongxin Xinxi Bao 通信信息报*, January 26, 2011, A06.
77. Chen Tian, "China Mobile Pushing Fetion," *Global Times*, July 9, 2013, accessed September 8, 2016, www.globaltimes.cn/content/794978.shtml; Yan Ma, Xia Liu, and Qiling Lin, "Liantong Tengxun lianshou tui Weixin" 联通腾讯联手推微信 [Unicom and Tencent to Jointly Promote Weixin], *Qiyejia Ribao 企业家日报*, July 22, 2013, 4.
78. Dong-Hee Shin, "What Makes Consumers Use VoIP Over Mobile Phones? Free Riding or Consumerization of New Service," *Telecommunications Policy* 36, no. 4 (2012): 311–23.
79. Shahrokh Nikou, Harry Bouwman, and Mark de Reuver, "The Potential of Converged Mobile Telecommunications Services: A Conjoint Analysis," *Info* 14, no. 5 (2012): 21–35; Aniruddha Banerjee, James Alleman, and Paul Rappoport, "Video-Viewing Behavior in the Era of Connected Devices," *Communications and Strategies* 92 (2013): 19–42.
80. Hu Hu, "Sanwang ronghe de lishixing tupo" 三网"融合的历史性突破 [A Historical Breakthrough of the Three-Network Convergence], *Renmin Youdian Bao 人民邮电报*, January 18, 2010, accessed February 3, 2017, www.chinaunicom.com.cn/news/ywsm/hyzx/file876.html.

81. Rangrang Bai and Guangwei Wang, "Jiegou chongzu guizhi zhihou yu zongxiang quanding—Zhongguo Dianxin Liantong fanlongduan anli de ruogan sikao" 结构重组、规制滞后与纵向圈定—中国电信、联通"反垄断"案例的若干思考 [Some Thoughts on the Anti-Monopoly Case Against China Telecom and Unicom], *China Industrial Economics* 10 (October 2012): 135–47; Zhan Hao and Annie Xue, "China Deregulates Pricing in Telecommunication Sector," *China Law Vision*, May 29, 2014, accessed September 8, 2016, www.chinalawvision.com/2014/05/articles/competitionantitrust-law-of-th/china-deregulates-pricing-in-telecommunication-sector/.
82. Hong, *Networking China*, 11.
83. Xiao Xu, "Duanxin yewu mianlin weixin chongji" 短信业务面临微信冲击 通讯巨头与运营商博弈日趋激烈 [Text Message Service Took a Hit from Weixin], *Gongren Ribao 工人日报*, March 20, 2013, 6.
84. Yan Ma, "Gongxinbu cheng you keneng dui Weixin shoufei" 工信部称有可能对微信收费 运营商态度各有不同 [MIIT May Consider Charging Weixin Service], *Securities Daily 证券日报*, April 1, 2013, C03.
85. Ibid.
86. Lirong Chen, "Zhongdianxin yu Tengxun gaodiao hezuo" 中电信与腾讯高调合作 移动互联网上演变革记 [China Telecom to Collaborate with Tencent], *Tongxin Xinxi Bao 通信信息报*, April 20, 2011, B03.
87. Ri Yao, "Dianxin lianhe Tengxun tui tianyi QQ haoma fuwu" 电信联合腾讯推天翼QQ号码服务 手机号即QQ号 [China Telecom and Tencent Jointly Promote E-Surfing QQ Number Service], *Tech.qq.com 腾讯科技*, November 1, 2011, accessed September 8, 2016, http://tech.qq.com/a/20111101/000010.htm.
88. Na Li and Jia Liu, "Tengxun gei Liantong fa Weixin" 腾讯给联通发微信：OTT 之争破冰求共赢 [Tencent and China Unicom to Collaborate with Weixin Service]," *China Business News 第一财经日报*, July 19, 2013, B04.
89. Tencent, Prospectus, 26.
90. Ibid., 89.
91. "QQ zuankuo leyuan" 钻阔乐园, "pandian Tengxun tingzhi yunying de youxi" 盘点腾讯停止运营的游戏 腾讯停运的游戏有哪些 [The Games Tencent No Longer Operating], n.p., July 17, 2016, accessed September 26, 2016, www.qqzuankuo.com/article/youxigonglue/2016061701061890.html.
92. "Tencent and Neowiz to Bring Online Rollerblade Racing Game 'R2Beat' in China," Financial Releases of 2005, *Tencent*, accessed September 26, 2016, www.tencent.com/en-us/news_timeline.html; Matt Martin, "Tencent to Manage Crytek's Warface in China," *gamesindustry.biz*, December 13, 2010, accessed September 26, 2016, www.gamesindustry.biz/articles/2010-12-13-tencent-to-manage-cryteks-warface-in-china; "Jianzhi TGA Lieyanxingdong xianshang yuxuan mingluo kaisai" 剑指TGA 《烈焰行动》线上预选鸣锣开赛 [Tencent to Launch Battery], n.p., April 18, 2013, accessed September 26, 2016, http://news.pcgames.com.cn/280/2806538.html; Eric Jou, "Check Out China's 'New' 'Genuine American-Style Zombie Shooting Game,'" n.p., June 5, 2013, accessed September 26, 2016, http://kotaku.com/check-out-chinas-new-genuine-american-style-zombie-493092880; "Our Story," *Vertigo Games*, accessed September 26, 2016, www.vertigogames.co.kr/#/; Teng Shi, "Tengxun daily Han 2D hengban QQ xianjing pingce" 腾讯代理韩2D横版《QQ仙境》评测 [Review on *QQ Xianjing*], *PCGames*, January 6, 2011, accessed September 26, 2016, http://news.pcgames.com.cn/ceping/guonei/1012/2088012_all.html; THR Staff, "Zynga Partners with Tencent in China for Chinese Version of Cityville," *Hollywood Reporter.com*, July 26, 2011, accessed June 28, 2014, LexisNexis Academic.

93. Charles Custer, "Game Developers: Want to Win in China? Partner with Tencent," *Tech in Asia*, February 25, 2014, accessed March 3, 2017, www.techinasia.com/the-key-to-foreign-game-success-in-china-partner-with-tencent.
94. Charles Custer, "How Tencent Is Taking Over Global Gaming," *Tech in Asia*, June 21, 2016, accessed September 26, 2016, www.techinasia.com/tencent-gaming-world.
95. Tencent, Interim Report, 2007, 19; "GoPets, Ltd. Continues Global Expansion, Achieving 300,000 Users Worldwide and Securing Singapore Partnership Deal," *PR Newswire*, April 25, 2006, accessed September 26, 2016, www.prnewswire.com/news-releases/gopets-ltd-continues-global-expansion-achieving-300000-users-worldwide-and-securing-singapore-partnership-deal-56543132.html.
96. Tencent, Annual Report, 2008, 118; 2009, 123.
97. Ibid., 132.
98. Ibid., 2011, 189; 2012, 176.
99. "Connected Transaction Purchase of Shares of Level Up," *Tencent*, January 19, 2012, accessed September 26, 2016, www.tencent.com/en-us/news_timeline.html.
100. "About Us," *Activision Blizzard*, accessed September 26, 2016, www.activisionblizzard.com/about-us.
101. "Multi-Year Agreement Joins One of the World's Biggest Interactive Entertainment Franchises with China's Largest Online Games Platform," Financial Releases, *Tencent*, July 3, 2012, accessed September 26, 2016, www.tencent.com/en-us/articles/802871466501124.pdf; Tencent, Annual Report, 2013, 150.
102. Joe Donnelly, "Tencent Wins Rights to Officially Release PUBG in China, Will 'Accord with Socialist Core Values'," *PC Gamer*, November 22, 2017, accessed January 10, 2019, www.pcgamer.com/tencent-wins-rights-to-officially-release-pubg-in-china-will-accord-with-socialist-core-values/.
103. Lynn T. Harrison, *Introduction to 3D Game Engine Design Using DirectX 9 and C#* (Berkeley, CA: Apress, 2003), 1.
104. Tencent, Annual Report, 2012, 133.
105. Ibid., 191.
106. "Riot Games and Tencent Ink Deal to Bring League of Legends to China," *Riot Games*, accessed September 26, 2016, www.riotgames.com/sites/default/files/uploads/081121_NEWS_lol_tencentchinarelease.pdf.
107. Tencent, Annual Report, 2010, 190.
108. "Tencent Holding Acquires Majority Stake in Game Publisher Riot Games," Financial Releases of 2011, *Tencent*, February 4, 2011, accessed September 26, 2016, www.tencent.com/en-us/news_timeline.html.
109. John Gaudiosi, "This Chinese Tech Giant Owns More Than Riot Games," *Fortune*, December 22, 2015, accessed September 26, 2016, http://fortune.com.
110. Catherine Shu, "Tencent Will Pay $126M for a 14.6% Stake in Glu Mobile, Maker of Kim Kardashian: Hollywood," *TechCrunch*, April 29, 2015, accessed September 26, 2016, https://techcrunch.com/2015/04/29/tencent-glu/.
111. George Stahl, "Tencent Buys Stake in Kardashian Game Maker Glu Mobile," *Wall Street Journal*, April 29, 2015, accessed September 26, 2016, www.wsj.com/articles/tencent-buys-stake-in-kardashian-game-maker-glu-mobile-1430344216.
112. Bien Perez, "China's Tencent Partners with Glu Mobile to Bring Popular WeFire Mobile Shooter Game to International Markets," *South China Morning Post*, November 6, 2015, accessed September 26, 2016, www.scmp.com/tech/apps-gaming/article/1876205/chinas-tencent-partners-glu-mobile-bring-popular-wefire-mobile.
113. Tencent, Annual Report, 2014, 143.

114. Jon Russell, "Tencent Confirms Deal to Buy Majority Stake in Supercell from SoftBank for $8.6B," *TechCrunch*, June 21, 2016, accessed September 26, 2016, https://techcrunch.com/2016/06/21/tencent-confirms-deal-to-buy-majority-stake-in-supercell-from-softbank-for-8-6b/.
115. Alibaba, Annual Report, 2015, 149–50, accessed September 26, 2016, www.alibabagroup.com/en/ir/secfilings.
116. "Tencent to Acquire Majority Stake in Supercell from SoftBank," Financial Release of 2016, *Tencent*, accessed September 26, 2016, www.tencent.com/en-us/news_timeline.html.
117. This is the earliest documented information I was able to trace. No such information was revealed in Tencent's IPO Prospectus. Tencent, Annual Report, 2004, 60.
118. Ibid., Annual Report, 2015, 133.
119. "Tencent Announces Launch of Int'l QQ," *Chinadaily.com.cn*, December 12, 2010, accessed March 3, 2017, www.chinadaily.com.cn/business/2010-12/16/content_11712170.htm.
120. "China's Tencent Launches English Microblogging Site," *AFP*, October 11, 2011.
121. Harsimran Julka, "China's Tencent Aims to Battle U.S. Web Firms like Google, Facebook in India," *Economic Times*, July 27, 2012; Suchit Leesanguansuk, "Tencent Launches Wechat Messaging App in Thailand," *Bangkok Post*, November 27, 2012.
122. "Tencent's WeChat Overseas Users Exceed 70 Million," *CRI Online*, July 5, 2013, accessed October 25, 2016, http://en.people.cn/90778/8311962.html.
123. Jon Russell, "Tencent Focuses on Indonesia with Local Joint Venture to Promote Its Wechat Mobile App," *Next Web*, February 28, 2013, accessed September 18, 2016, http://thenextweb.com/asia/2013/02/28/tencent-focuses-on-indonesia-with-local-joint-venture-to-promote-its-wechat-mobile-app/.
124. Steven Millward, "WeChat's Global Expansion Has Been a Disaster," *Tech in Asia*, May 25, 2016, accessed October 25, 2016, www.techinasia.com/wechat-global-expansion-fail.
125. Paul Mozur, "China's Tencent Aims App at Mobile Users in the U.S.," *Wall Street Journal Asia*, March 6, 2013, 17.
126. "WeChat Payment Fully Open to Overseas Purchase," *Xinhua*, November 20, 2015, accessed October 25, 2016, http://news.xinhuanet.com/english/2015-11/20/c_134838085.htm.
127. Scott Duke Harris, "S.F. Firm Gets China Investor," *Mercury News*, January 9, 2008, accessed November 20, 2016, www.mercurynews.com/2008/01/09/s-f-firm-gets-china-investor/.
128. Scott Cendrowski, "Tencent's Venture Capital: Huge in China, Invisible in America," *Fortune*, July 22, 2015, accessed March 3, 2017, http://fortune.com/2015/07/22/tencents-venture-capital-us/.
129. Zhang Zhao, "Action Rolls as Online Portals Sign on with US Movie Giants," *China Daily European Edition*, January 30, 2013; Patrick Brzeski, "Chinese Internet Giant Tencent Licenses Disney Films for Streaming Video Service," *Hollywood Reporter.com*, September 9, 2013; Tencent, "Financial Releases," 2014–2015, www.tencent.com/en-us/news_timeline.html; Paul Melvin, "Tencent Joins Hands with ESPN in Exclusive Digital Partnership in China," *ESPN Media Zone*, February 2, 2016, accessed September 18, 2016, http://espnmediazone.com/us/press-releases/2016/02/tencent-joins-hands-with-espn-in-exclusive-digital-partnership-in-china/.

Conclusion

Tencent, a China-based global Internet giant, as an intersection reveals the dynamics and interactions between the two poles of growth in the global political economy—China and the Internet.

Tencent has emerged in a historical context—primarily domestic but also global. Tracing through the discourse and rhetoric changes in the numerous policies the Chinese government issued and the nation's social-economic performance as the outcomes of these policies shows that China's Internet has gone through four developmental stages. The Internet transformed from an infrastructure network that facilitated national economy in agrarian and industrial growth to a pillar industry itself that (re)shaped the political-economic epicenter surrounding ICT businesses. Tencent's economic profile, particularly its expansion strategies, reveals it as highly integrated, both horizontally and vertically, and diversified. In its ownership and control, Tencent has been substantially transnationalized in terms of corporate governance and institutional connections. Tencent's transnationalization is further demonstrated by its extensive influences in global cultural sphere via popular products such as QQ, WeChat, and gaming. The four chapters show how Tencent, as an epitome of the larger transformation in China's Internet industry, has been integrated and transnationalized with the joint efforts of state entities and units of domestic and transitional capital.

Contextualizing Tencent Within China's Internet History

The first contribution of this book is identifying the four historical periods of China's Internet development. The first stage was between 1987 and 1993 when various science and technology research entities initiated research on computer networks. After China established the first full Internet operation under TCP/IP protocol in 1994, the nation's Internet building entered a second stage. In 1994 and 1995, an enormous amount of effort and money was put into constructing the information infrastructures to facilitate the industrial growth. Some high-profile projects are the China Education and Research Network (CERNET), ChinaNet, and the Golden Projects. A third stage witnessed an intensive development in the Internet and ICT industry between 1996 and 2010. With the further opening up of the domestic market to private capital and, especially, foreign capital, many private companies in Internet value-added services emerged, among which were some well-known names: Alibaba, Baidu, JD, NetEase, Sina, Sohu, and Tencent. This stage also paralleled the Internet boom in the United States, where newly established technology companies were springing up for initial public offerings on the stock exchange markets. The fourth period responded to the 2007–8 global financial crisis and saw the Internet industry elevate to a pillar industry in China's economic development. While this is still ongoing, a recent "Internet Plus" strategy aims at integrating the Internet into all aspects of the national political economy and building a networked Chinese society.[1]

History clearly shows that China's Internet development was highly state driven. Contrary to the conventional belief that the Chinese government has been a holdback, it actually has stood on the forefront of commercializing the ICT sector. State policies were made to liberalize the domestic market where private capital assumed significant roles in the Internet industry. In addition, state entities at various levels were reorganized in ways that facilitated the efficient leadership and coordination on matters of industrialization and informatization.

The rise of Tencent is a story of the state and private capital. Tencent emerged at a time private capital and foreign investors were encouraged to build a Chinese Internet industry.

A Transnational Tencent

Transnational capital also was significant in Tencent's evolvement and ownership structure. The China-based, transnational Internet company has incorporated transnational elements since its early stages. In the first two years of Tencent's establishment, it received investment from U.S.-backed IDG Ventures China (IDG Capital), Hong Kong-based PCCW, and South Africa-based MIH. Naspers, MIH's parent company and a South Africa-based multinational media conglomerate, is still Tencent's primary institutional stakeholder as of December 2018 with up to 33.10 percent of shares.[2] In view of this capital structure and corporate governance, Tencent is a transnational Internet company almost by creation.

Owing partly to its global stakeholders and partly to expansion strategies, Tencent's businesses have been highly transnationalized. Tencent has successfully expanded into South and Southeast Asia, South America, Europe, and North America through service provision, research and development, joint ventures, mergers and acquisitions, and strategic partnerships. Revenues from overseas markets have grown steadily and substantially since 2010. Tencent, through horizontal and vertical integration, is a major player in the global game industry.

Tencent is only one case of China's burgeoning Internet companies. Such industry champions as Alibaba, Baidu, JD, NetEase, Qihoo363, and Sohu to different extents have incorporated transnational elements in their business and capital structures. This suggests a need in shifting questions from "how the Internet will change China" to "how China will change the global Internet."[3]

An Integrated Tencent

The case study of Tencent shows that China's Internet industry is multi-faced and much broader than the simple production and provision of Internet access, content, and value. Not only has the Internet industry redefined social relations and online and offline lifestyles but, more critically, it also continued reshaping forms of production, distribution, and consumption. It has done so through horizontal and vertical integration, diversification, and transnationalization. This is a third contribution of the book.

The massive Tencent empire encompassed various aspects of Internet and broadly defined media and communication services. Tencent first started with diversifying its businesses within the realm of online and mobile value-added services and gradually made investments in other companies that allowed it to horizontally and vertically integrate in various markets. Since 2010, a more comprehensive and encompassing expansion strategy has matured as Tencent extended control into the broadly defined communication and cultural industry as well as more diversified businesses.

These features displayed by Tencent are in no way unique to Chinese Internet industry. Not only can similar traits of expansion be found in previous political-economy studies of Alibaba and Google and other U.S. Internet companies, but also these processes and strategies are consistent with what has been observed in media and communication industries over decades. In a more fundamental sense, the Internet industry has the business nature of any other capitalist industry, where the processes of concentration, commodification, and commercialization have been governing. It contributes to the growing trends of consumerism, commercialism, and digital capitalism that have dominated both Western societies and China's growing consumer society.

Even more so, the Internet industry has been in alliances with many other powerful corporate players, such as the banks and financial institutions, as well as those public institutions that have been increasingly privatized, including education, research, and health care, among others.

The Internet as a Site to (Re)conceptualize State-Capital Relations

A fourth contribution is a theoretical reconceptualization of the role of the state in the political economy of Internet studies. The development of Tencent needs to be understood in light of general economic and political contexts in and outside China, which entails regulations and deregulations on Internet industry, China's market transformations and global reintegration, and the expansion of transnational digital capitalism.

Tencent's successful commodification strategies with QQ and WeChat show that the central state has been actively making room for Internet capital to develop aggressively; the state did so by balancing, and to some extent limiting, the power of the telecommunication giants that used to be national champions. Such a protective and encouraging attitude to domestic Internet companies is also consistent with what Dan Schiller has observed in Chinese government's approach to U.S.-based global Internet giants: "Although China's party-controlled state welcomed unprecedented quantities of foreign direct investment into many industries, it was also impressively successful in setting terms of entry into the national market for the strategic communications and information sector."[4] While Google, Facebook, Apple, and Amazon have taken over most of the market in the rest of world, their Chinese counterparts—Alibaba, Baidu, and Tencent—still dominate the Chinese territory. These are indebted to the more constituting and encouraging than restraining role of the Chinese state.

Reflections on Transnationalization and Financialization

Two emergent dynamics need to be further clarified: the Internet industry in the Global South countries—particularly, the emerging economies, such as Brazil, Russia, India, China, and South Africa (BRICS)—and the relations between the ICT industry and global financial sector.

The Chinese Internet industry—with Tencent being just one case—has been in active interactions with the digital industries from the emerging economies. While much ink has been spilled over the rising "locomotives of the South"—the BRICS countries—as vectors of change in the global economy, the unique pattern of interactions in their digital industries remains understudied.[5] The political economy of the Internet industry in BRICS is significant not only to the understanding of the global ICT network but also to the changing geopolitics of information, which have been traditionally dominated by the United States and its allies in the Western world.

How much room does global capitalism hold for the rising Internet capital from BRICS? To what extent are the BRICS countries competing or collaborating with the existing leading players from the United States and Western Europe? In what ways does BRICS stand as an analytical unit that contributes to an updated understanding of global political economy? More than 15 years after the term "BRIC" was initially coined, a decade after the first BRIC summit was held, and five years after the BRICS development bank was proposed, these questions still sit unanswered. More important, the questions whether and to what extent BRICS would function as another unit of geopolitical power are acquiring new urgency in a drastically changing international political environment where North America, Europe, and the Middle East are witnessing uncertainties in their own ways.

Two critical tasks arise from these questions: to analyze the interconnections in portfolio investors, business sectors, suppliers, customers, managerial personnel, and human resources of the BRICS Internet companies, and, to map out the network among them. Building on the academic discussion of digital capitalism and global Internet governance, such a project would add knowledge about the geopolitics of information from the perspective of the Global South countries.

Also revealed in this book is an interweaving relationship between the global ICT industry and financial sector, as contemporary neoliberal ramifications. While initial growth of the Internet companies was heavily dependent on the participation of financial capital, a latest development saw a great number of technology companies become venture-capital investors themselves and participate in ICT investments.

In light of the critical role of venture capital in global ICT, the history, development, and regulations of it have yet been sufficiently investigated. This includes a set of questions: Since when and in what ways has venture capital come into being? How have the forms of venture capitalist investments in ICT industry evolved and varied in the United States and globally? Who are the primary stakeholders in venture capital, and how might these people's social economic capital inform their investments? What is the role of state in the development of venture capital investments and transnational digital industry? What, if any, are the regulatory considerations regarding the use of venture capital in ICT sectors, and to what extent have these concerns been articulated? What power has venture capital exercised over Internet system development?

These questions speak to three interrelated, understudied aspects in the processes of transnational capitalist expansion in technology industry: the development of independent venture capital firms, such as Sequoia Capital, in the context of the rise of Silicon Valley; the evolvement of venture-capital arms in traditional major investment banks, such as Goldman Sachs's venture capital and growth equity team; and the growth of venture-capital organizations within the Internet industry itself, such as IDG Ventures. To trace the histories of these three types of entities and to analyze the political-economic contexts that have enabled and conditioned their development would demonstrate how the participation of venture capital investments has further consolidated and accelerated the private actors' dominance over the provision system of global communication and information.

Foregrounding the ICT sector as an important and ever-burgeoning vehicle for global capitalist expansion orchestrated by the neoliberal states and private capital, the intertwined relations between global financial and ICT sectors not only stand as a vector of contemporary social changes but also shed light on the trajectory of the global financial and digital capitalism. Christian Fuchs notes about the relation between information economy and crisis that

> capitalism is not only an imperialistic system that appropriates, expropriates and exploits spaces, humans and resources to perpetuate its existence and create and reproduce spheres of capital accumulation but also . . . a crisis-ridden system. Capital accumulation again and again reaches certain limits and enters phases where its own antagonisms explode and create situations of economic crisis.[6]

To make sense of where the current ICT system leads and what crisis and/or opportunities lie ahead is perhaps an ongoing intellectual puzzle, the solution to which can only be rooted in looking back and understanding the history.

Notes

1. Hong, *Networking China*, 144–46.
2. Tencent, Annual Report, 2015, 62.
3. Shen, "Across the Great (Fire) Wall," 254–55.
4. D. Schiller, *Digital Depression*, 231.
5. Vijay Prashad, *The Poorer Nations: A Possible History of the Global South* (London: Verso, 2012).
6. Fuchs, *Foundations*, 221.

Bibliography

Arrighi, Giovanni. *Adam Smith in Beijing: Lineages of the Twenty-First Century*. London: Verso, 2007.

Atherton, Andrew, and Alaric Fairbanks. "Stimulating Private Sector Development in China: The Emergence of Enterprise Development Centres in Liaoning and Sichuan Provinces." *Asia Pacific Business Review* 12, no. 3 (2006): 333–54.

Banerjee, Aniruddha, James Alleman, and Paul Rappoport. "Video-Viewing Behavior in the Era of Connected Devices." *Communications and Strategies* 92 (2013): 19–42.

Barabantseva, Elena. "In Pursuit of an Alternative Model? The Modernisation Trap in China's Official Development Discourse." *East Asia* 29, no. 1 (2012): 63–79.

Bodnaruk, Andriy, Massimo Massa, and Andrei Simonov. "Investment Banks as Insiders and the Market for Corporate Control." *Review of Financial Studies* 22, no. 12 (2009): 4989–5026.

Cao, Yong, and John D. H. Downing. "The Realities of Virtual Play: Video Games and Their Industry in China." *Media, Culture, & Society* 30, no. 4 (2008): 515–29.

Casey, Carolyn P. "The 1986 Provisions to Encourage Foreign Investment in China: Further Evolution in Chinese Investment Laws." *American University International Law Review* 2, no. 2 (1987): 579–614.

Chakravartty, Paula, and Yuezhi Zhao. "Toward a Transcultural Political Economy of Global Communication." In *Global Communication: Toward a Transcultural Political Economy*, edited by Paula Chakravartty and Yuezhi Zhao, 1–19. Lanham, MD: Rowman and Littlefield, 2008.

Chang, Heng-Hao, and Alvin Y. So. "Powerful Communist Party, Robust Capitalist Economy: Interpreting the Chinese Puzzle." *Humboldt Journal of Social Relations* 24, no. 1–2 (1998): 101–27.

Chen, Xiangming, and Ahmed Kanna. *Rethinking Global Urbanism: Comparative Insights from Secondary Cities*. New York: Routledge, 2012.

Chen, Yaohua, Lijun Sheng, and Di Pan. *"Jinrong qiye rongtouzi celue yu caozuo"* *金融企业融投资策略与操作 [Strategies and Operations of Financing and Investment for Financial Enterprises]*. Beijing: China Industry and Commerce, 2005.

Crain, Matthew. "Financial Markets and Online Advertising: Reevaluating the Dotcom Investment Bubble." *Information, Communication, & Society* 17, no. 3 (2014): 371–84.

———. "The Revolution Will Be Commercialized: Finance, Public Policy, and the Construction of Internet Advertising." PhD diss., Communications, University of Illinois, Urbana-Champaign, 2013.

Dang, Haoqi. "Cong chuanboxue jiaodu jiegou weixin de xinxi chuanbo moshi" 从传播学角度解构微信的信息传播模式 [A Communication Approach to Understand the Model of Wexin]. *Southeast Communication* 7 (2012): 71–78.

Danielian, Noobar R. *AT&T: The Story of Industrial Conquest*. New York: Vanguard, 1939.

Foster, John Bellamy, and Robert W. McChesney. *The Endless Crisis: How Monopoly-Finance Capital Produces Stagnation and Upheaval from the USA to China*. New York: Monthly Review, 2012.

Foster, John Bellamy, Robert W. McChesney, and R. Jamil Jonna. "The Global Reserve Army of Labor and the New Imperialism." *Monthly Review* 63, no. 6 (2011): 1–31.

Fuchs, Christian. *Foundations of Critical Media and Information Studies*. London: Routledge, 2011.

Golding, Peter, and Graham Murdock. "Theories of Communication and Theories of Society." *Communication Research* 5, no. 3 (1978): 339–56.

Hachgian, Nina. "China's Cyber-Strategy." *Foreign Affairs* (March–April 2001): 118–33.

Han, Kyun-Tae. "Composition of Board of Directors of Major Media Corporations." *Journal of Media Economics* 1, no. 2 (1988): 85–100.

Harrison, Lynn T. *Introduction to 3D Game Engine Design Using DirectX 9 and C#*. Berkeley, CA: Apress, 2003.

Harvey, David. *A Brief History of Neoliberalism*. Oxford: Oxford University Press, 2005.

Harwit, Eric. *China's Telecommunication Revolution*. New York: Oxford University Press, 2008.

Harwit, Eric, and Jack Su. "A Telecom Newcomer Challenges the MPT Monopoly." *China Business Review* 23, no. 6 (1996): 22–23.

Herman, Edward S. *Corporate Control, Corporate Power*. Cambridge: Cambridge University Press, 1981.

Herman, Edward S., and Robert W. McChesney. *The Global Media: The New Missionaries of Corporate Capitalism*. London: Cassell, 1997.

Hong, Yu. *Labor, Class Formation, and China's Informationized Policy of Economic Development*. Lanham, MD: Lexington, 2011.

———. *Networking China*. Urbana-Champaign: University of Illinois Press, 2017.

———. "Pivot to Internet Plus: Molding China's Digital Economy for Economic Restructuring?" *International Journal of Communication* 11 (2017): 1486–506.

———. "Reading the Twelfth Five-Year Plan: China's Communication-Driven Mode of Economic Restructuring." *International Journal of Communication* 5 (2011): 1045–57.

———. "Repurposing Telecoms for Capital in China." *Asian Survey* 53, no. 2 (2013): 319–47.

Hsu, S. Philip, Yu-Shan Wu, and Suisheng Zhao, eds. *In Search of China's Development Model: Beyond the Beijing Consensus*. London: Routledge, 2011.

Jia, Lianrui, and Dwayen Winseck. "The Political Economy of Chinese Internet Companies: Financializaton, Concentration, and Capitalization." *International Communication Gazette* (2018), Vol. 80, Issue. 1: 30–59.

Jin, Dal Yong. "Critical Analysis of User Commodities as Free Labour in Social Networking Sites: A Case Study of Cyworld." *Continuum* 29, no. 6 (2015): 938–50.

———. *Korea's Online Gaming Empire*. Boston: MIT Press, 2010.

———. "Neoliberal Restructuring of the Global Communication System: Mergers and Acquisitions." *Media, Culture, & Society* 30, no. 3 (2008): 357–73.

Lardy, Nicholas R. *Markets Over Mao: The Rise of Private Business in China*. Washington, DC: Peterson Institute for International Economics, 2014.

Lee, Chin-Chuan, Zhou He, and Yu Huang. "Chinese Party Publicity Inc. Conglomerated: The Case of the Shenzhen Press Group." *Media, Culture & Society* 28, no. 4 (2006).

Li, Minqi. *The Rise of China and the Demise of the Capitalist World-Economy*. New York: Monthly Review, 2008.

Liao, Annie, Clyde Eirikur Hull, and Rajendran Sriramachandramurthy. "The Six Facets Model of Technology Management: A Study in the Digital Business Industry." *International Journal of Innovation & Technology Management* 10, no. 4 (2013): 1–24.

Lin, Chun. *China and Global Capitalism: Reflections on Marxism, History, and Contemporary Politics*. New York: Palgrave Pivot, 2013.

Lin, Jun. *"Feiteng Shiwu nian: China's Internet 1995–2009" 沸腾十五年：中国互联网1995–2009 [The Hustle and Bustle of China's Internet: Fifteen Years Between 1995–2009]*. Beijing: China Citic, 2009.

Lin, Jun, and Yuezhou Zhang. *"Ma Huateng de Tengxun Diguo" 马化腾的腾讯帝国 [Ma Huateng's Tencent Empire]*. Beijing: China Citic, 2009.

Liu, Bih Jane, and Yu-Yin Wu. "Development Zones in China: Are STIPs a Substitute for or a Complement to ETDZs?" *Taipei Economic Inquiry* 47, no. 1 (2011): 97–145.

Livingstone, Sonia. "Taking Risky Opportunities in Youthful Content Creation: Teenagers' Use of Social Networking Sites for Intimacy, Privacy, and Self-Expression." *New Media & Society* 10, no. 3 (2008): 393–411.

Lovelock, Peter, Theodore C. Clark, and Ben A. Petrazzini. "The 'Golden Projects': China's National Networking Initiative." *Information Infrastructure & Policy* 5, no. 4 (1996): 265–77.

Lu, Benfu, and Junlan Zhou. "Gongxiang jingji de chuangye dachao he shangye moshi fenxi" 共享经济的创业大潮和商业模式分析 [An Analysis on the Sharing Economy and Its Business Model]. In *Legalization of Cyberspace: Annual Report of Internet and State Governance 2015*, edited by Zhian Zhang, 127–36. Beijing: Commercial, 2015.

Lu, Ding. "China's Telecommunications Infrastructure Buildup: On Its Own Way." In *Deregulation and Interdependence in the Asia-Pacific Region*, edited by Takatoshi Ito and Anne O. Krueger, 371–413. Chicago: University of Chicago Press, 2000.

McChesney, Robert. *Communication Revolution: Critical Junctures and the Future of Media*. New York: New Press, 2007.

———. *Digital Disconnect: How Capitalism Is Turning the Internet Against Democracy*. New York: New Press, 2013.

McIntyre, Bryce T. "Let a Hundred Modems Bloom: The Internet in Today's China." In *Cyberpath to Development in Asia: Issues and Challenges*, edited by Sandhya Rao and Bruce C. Klopfenstein, 63–84. Westport, CT: Praeger, 2002.

McMillan, Sally J., and Jang-sun Hwang. "Nailing Jell-O to the Wall and Herding Cats: A Content Analysis of Chinese and U.S. Newspaper Coverage of the Internet in China." *Journal of Intercultural Communication Research* 31, no. 2 (2002): 107–25.

Miglo, Anton, Zhenting Lee, and Shuting Liang. "Capital Structure of Internet Companies: Case Study." *Journal of Internet Commerce* 13, no. 3–4 (2014): 253–81.

Mosco, Vincent. *The Political Economy of Communication: Rethinking and Renewal*. London: Sage, 2009.

———. *To the Cloud: Big Data in a Turbulent World*. Boulder, CO: Paradigm, 2014.

———. "Toward a Theory of the State and Telecommunications Policy." *Journal of Communication* 38, no. 1 (1988): 107–24.

Mueller, Milton L., and Wolter Lemstra. "Liberalization and the Internet." In *International Handbook of Network Industries: The Liberalization of Infrastructure*, edited by Matthias Finger and Rolf W. Kunneke, 144–61. Cheltenham: Elgar, 2011.

Mueller, Milton L., and Zixiang Tan. *China in the Information Age: Telecommunications and the Dilemmas of Reform*. Westport, CT: Praeger, 1997.

Murdock, Graham, and Peter Golding. "For a Political Economy of Mass Communications." *Socialist Register* 10 (1973): 205–34.

Nederveen Pieterse, Jan. "Representing the Rise of the Rest as Threat." *Global Media & Communication* 5, no. 2 (2009): 221–37.

Nikou, Shahrokh, Harry Bouwman, and Mark de Reuver. "The Potential of Converged Mobile Telecommunications Services: A Conjoint Analysis." *Info* 14, no. 5 (2012): 21–35.

Ning, Ping. "OICQ xue Disini yaoguo sandao kan" QICQ学迪斯尼要过三道坎 [OICQ Has to Overcome Three Difficulties Like Disney]. *China Business Journal*, April 17, 2001, 2.

Nolan, Peter. *Is China Buying the World*. Malden, MA: Polity, 2012.

Orleans, Leo A. *Science in Contemporary China*. Stanford, CA: Stanford University Press, 1980.

Prashad, Vijay. *The Poorer Nations: A Possible History of the Global South*. London: Verso, 2012.

Qiu, Jack Linchuan. *Working-Class Network Society: Communication Technology and the Information Have-Less in Urban China*. Cambridge, MA: MIT Press, 2009.

Sandberg, Jaredet. "Net Gain." *Newsweek*, December 7, 1998, 46.

Schiller, Dan. *Digital Capitalism: Networking the Global Market System*. Cambridge, MA: MIT Press, 1999.

———. *Digital Depression: Information Technology and Economic Crisis*. Urbana-Champaign: University of Illinois Press, 2014.

———. *How to Think About Information*. Urbana-Champaign: University of Illinois Press, 2007.

———. "Poles of Market Growth: Open Question About China, Information, and the World Economy." *Global Media and Communication* 1, no. 1 (2005): 79–103.

Schiller, Herbert. *Information and the Crisis Economy*. Norwood, NJ: Ablex, 1984.

Shambaugh, David. *China Goes Global: The Partial Power*. Oxford: Oxford University Press, 2013.

Shapiro, Carl, and Hai R. Varian. *Information Rules: A Strategic Guide to the Network Economy*. Boston: Harvard Business, 1999.

Shen, Hong. "Across the Great (Fire) Wall: China and the Global Internet." PhD diss., Communications, University of Illinois, Urbana-Champaign, 2017.

Shen, Jianfa. "Urban Growth and Sustainable Development in Shenzhen City 1980–2006." *Open Environmental Journal* 2 (2008): 71–79.

Shi, Zhong-Liang. "Outline of the Ninth Five-Year Plan for National Economic and Social Development and the Long-Term Goals to the Year 2010." In *China's Transition to a Socialist Market Economy*, edited by Mohamed Osman Suliman. Westport, CT: Quorum, 1998.

Shin, Dong-Hee. "What Makes Consumers Use VoIP Over Mobile Phones? Free Riding or Consumerization of New Service." *Telecommunications Policy* 36, no. 4 (2012): 311–23.

Shirk, Susan. *Changing Media, Changing China*. New York: Oxford University Press, 2011.

Sirois, André, and Janet Wasko. "The Political Economy of the Recorded Music Industry: Redefinitions and New Trajectories in the Digital Age." In *The Handbook of Political Economy of Communications*, edited by Janet Wasko, Graham Murdock, and Helena Sousa, 331–57. Chichester: Wiley-Blackwell, 2011.

Smythe, Dallas Walker. "On the Political Economy of Communications." *Journalism & Mass Communication Quarterly* 37 (1960): 563–72.

So, Alvin Y. "Rethinking the Chinese Developmental Miracle." In *China and the Transformation of Global Capitalism*, edited by Ho-fung Huang, 50–64. Baltimore: John Hopkins University Press, 2009.

Tai, Qiuqing. "China's Media Censorship: A Dynamic and Diversified Regime." *Journal of East Asian Studies* 14 (2014): 185–209.

Tan, Zixiang. "Regulating China's Internet: Convergence Toward a Coherent Regulatory Regime." *Telecommunications Policy* 23 (1999): 261–76.

Tan, Zixiang (Alex), William Foster, and Seymour Goodman. "China's State-Coordinated Internet Infrastructure." *Communications of the ACM* 42, no. 6 (1999): 44–52.

Toth, Latzko. "Metaphors of Synchrony: Emergence and Differentiation of Online Chat Devices." *Bulletin of Science, Technology, and Society* 30, no. 5 (2010): 362–74.

Tse, Edward. *China's Disruptors: How Alibaba, Xiaomi, Tencent, and Other Companies Are Changing the Rules of Business*. New York: Portfolio, 2015.

———. "Competing on the Edge: Chinese Conglomerates and Changes in Business Strategy." *China Business Review*, July 2015, 1.

Wang, Jing. " 'Stir-Frying' Internet Finance: Financialization and the Institutional Role of Financial News in China." *International Journal of Communication* 11 (2017): 581–602.

Wang, Shijie. “Guanyu Weixin yingxiao xianzhuang ji duice de sikao” 关于微信营销现状及对策的思考 [Some Thoughts on the Status and Strategies of Weixin Marketing]. *China Computer and Communication* 1 (2014): 111–13.

Wasko, Janet. *Hollywood in the Information Age: Beyond the Silver Screen*. Austin: University of Texas Press, 1995.

———. *Understanding Disney: The Manufacture of Fantasy*. Cambridge: Polity, 2001.

Wei, Xie. “Acquisition of Technological Capability Through Special Economic Zones (SEZs): The Case of Shenzhen SEZ.” *Industry and Innovation* 7, no. 2 (2000): 199–221.

Wong, John. *The Political Economy of Deng's Nanxun: Breakthrough in China's Reform and Development*. Hackensack, NJ: World Scientific, 2014.

Wong, Kwan-Yiu. “China's Special Economic Zone Experiment: An Appraisal.” Series B, Human Geography. *Geografiska Annaler* 69, no. 1 (1987): 27–40.

Workneh, Tewodrow W. “Sub-Saharan Africa.” In *Global Media Giants*, edited by Benjamin J. Birkinbine, Rodrigo Gomez, and Janet Wasko, 287–311. New York: Routledge, 2017.

Wu, Wei. “Great Leap or Long March: Some Policy Issues of the Development of the Internet in China.” *Telecommunications Policy* 20, no. 9 (1996): 699–711.

Wu, Xiaobo. *A Biography of Tencent*. Zhejiang, China: Zhejiang University Press, 2016.

Yang, Dali L. *Remaking the Chinese Leviathan: Market Transition and the Politics of Governance in China*. Stanford: Stanford University Press, 2004.

Yeo, ShinJoung. “Behind the Search Box: The Political Economy of a Global Internet Industry.” PhD diss., Library and Information Science, University of Illinois, Urbana-Champaign, 2014.

Yeo, Yukyung. “Remaking the Chinese State and the Nature of Economic Governance? The Early Appraisal of the 2008 ‘Super-Ministry’ Reform.” *Journal of Contemporary China* 18, no. 62 (2009): 729–43.

Yeung, Yue-man, Joanna Lee, and Gordon Kee. “China's Special Economic Zones at 30.” *Eurasian Geography and Economics* 50, no. 2 (2009): 222–40.

Yu, Guomin. “Hulianwang shi gaowei meijie: Yizhong shehui chuanbo gouzao de quanxin fanshi—Guanyu xianjieduan chuanmei fazhan ruogan lilun yu shijian wenti de bianzheng” 互联网是高维媒介：一种社会传播构造的全新范式—关于现阶段传媒发展若干理论与实践问题的辩证 [Internet Is High-Dimensional Media: A Brand-New Paradigm of Social Communication Construction—A Dialectical View of Current Theory and Practice]. In *Legalization of Cyberspace: Annual Report of Internet and State Governance 2015*, edited by Zhian Zhang, 209–17. Beijing: Commercial, 2015.

Yuan, Wenli. “E-Democracy@China: Does It Work?” *Chinese Journal of Communication* 3, no. 4 (2010): 488–503.

Zeitlin, Maurice. “Corporate Ownership and Control: The Large Corporation and the Capitalist Class.” *American Journal of Sociology* 79, no. 5 (1974): 1073–19.

Zeng, Qian. “Zhongguo Hulianwang jiandu zhengce fenxi (1994–2014): Yizhong kaifaxing weiquan zhuyi” 中国互联网监督政策分析(1994–2014)：一种开发型威权主义 [Analysis on Chinese Internet Regulation Policies (1994–2014): A Developmental Authoritarianism]. In *Legalization of Cyberspace: Annual*

Report of Internet and State Governance 2015, edited by Zhian Zhang, 160–70. Beijing: Commercial, 2015.

Zhang, Junjie. "Zhongguo Hulianwang qiye fazhan moshi tanxi—yi Tengxun weili" 中国互联网企业发展模式探析—以腾讯为例 [Exploring Chinese Internet Companies' Developing Model—A Case Study on Tencent]. *Economy and Management* 2 (2011): 43–46.

Zhang, Lize. "The Survival and Development of Chinese New Media Business: Among State, Market, and Public." Master's thesis, National University of Singapore, Singapore, 2016.

Zhang, Shixin Ivy. *Impact of Globalization on the Local Press in China: A Case Study of the Beijing Youth Daily*. Lanham, MD: Lexington, 2014.

Zhang, Zhian, ed. *Legalization of Cyberspace: Annual Report of Internet and State Governance 2015*. Beijing: Commercial, 2015.

Zhao, Suisheng. "Deng Xiaoping's Southern Tour: Elite Politics in Post-Tiananmen China." *Asian Survey* 33, no. 8 (1993): 739–56.

Zhao, Yuezhi. "The Challenge of China: Contribution to a Transcultural Political Economy of Communication for the Twenty-First Century." In *The Handbook of Political Economy of Communication*, edited by Janet Wasko, Graham Murdock, and Helena Sousa, 558–82. Chichester: Wiley-Blackwell, 2011.

———. "China's Pursuits of Indigenous Innovations in Information Technology Developments: Hopes, Follies, and Uncertainties." *Chinese Journal of Communication* 3, no. 3 (2011): 266–89.

———. *Communication in China: Political Economy, Power, and Conflict*. Lanham, MD: Rowman and Littlefield, 2008.

———. *Media, Market, and Democracy in China: Between the Party Line and the Bottom Line*. Urbana-Champaign: University of Illinois Press, 1998.

———. "Neoliberal Strategies, Socialism Legacies: Communication and State Transformation in China." In *Global Communication: Toward a Transcultural Political Economy*, edited by Paula Chakravartty and Yuezhi Zhao, 23–50. Lanham, MD: Rowman and Littlefield, 2008.

Zhao, Yuezhi, and Dan Schiller. "Dances with Wolves? China's Integration into Digital Capitalism." *Info* 3, no. 2 (2001): 137–51.

Zheng, Cindy. "Opening the Digital Door: Computer Networking in China." *Telecommunications Policy* 18, no. 3 (1994): 236–42.

Zheng, Yongnian. *Globalization and State Transformation in China*. Cambridge: Cambridge University Press, 2004.

Zou, Haibo. "Tengxun shichang celue fenxi" 腾讯市场策略分析 [An Analysis of Tencent's Market Strategy]. *Modern Information* 5 (2005): 201–6.

Index

Note: **Boldface** page references indicate tables. *Italic* references indicate figures.

ABSA Bank Ltd. 68
Activision Blizzard 95
Alibaba 9, 43, 47, 49, 77, 110–11; Alibaba Group 52; Alibaba Pictures Group Ltd. 52
Alipay 49
Amazon 111
America Online (AOL) 33–34
Apple 1, 111
AutoNavi 47

Baidu 42, 47, 111
banking service of Tencent 51
Barclay's Africa Group 68
Beijing BIZCOM Technology Co. Ltd. 46
Beijing Media Corporation 74
Beijing Olympic Games (2008) 41
Beijing Starsinhand Technology Co. Ltd. 46
Board of Directors of Tencent (2004–18) **70**
Boda China 46
Brazil, Russia, India, China, and South Africa (BRICS) 111–12
bulletin board systems (BBS) of Tencent 46
business-to-business-to-consumer (B2B2C) 43
Buy.qq.com 43

Call of Duty game 95
CDMA technology 91
Central Leading Group for Cyberspace Affairs 16
Chaoxin 91
Cheetah Technology Corp. Ltd. 48
Chen Yidan 23, 33, 63
children's games of Tencent 87
China Education and Research Network (CERNET) 12, 109
China Information Security Evaluation Center 43
China Mobile 34, 90–2
China Music Corp. 88
ChinaNET 12–13, 20, 109
Chinapage 20
China Reading Ltd. 87
China South City Holdings Ltd. 49
China Telecom (formerly Directorate General of Telecommunications) 13, 90–1, 93
China United Telecommunications Corp. (China Unicom) 16, 34, 90–91
ChinaVision Media Group Ltd. 52
Chinese Academy of Sciences 9, 12, 14
Chinese Academy of Sciences network (CASNET) 12
Chinese FidoNet (CFido) 63
Cisco 85
CITIC Capital Holdings Ltd. 51
Cityville game 94
Clash of the Clans game 87, 96
Commission of Science, Technology, and Industry for National Defense 16
commodification 40
communication sector, Chinese 3–5; *see also* information and communication technology (ICT)
communications platforms of Tencent 40

Comsenz Group 46
corporate structure of Tencent 33–5, **33**, *35*
CrossFire game 86–7
Crytek 94
customer-to-customer (C2C) auction platform 43
Cyberspace Administration of China 16

Deng Xiaoping 1, 11, 24
Dianping.com 49
Didi Chuxing 76
Didi Dache 48–49
digital capitalism 93
digital mapping of Tencent 50–1
Digital Sky Technologies Ltd. 75
Ding Lei 20–1, 63
diversification 40, 51–3
dual-track ownership system in China 74
Dungeon and Fighter (DNF) game 86

e-commerce of Tencent 43, 47–8
economic and technological development zones (ETDZs) 22
E-House 50
Electronic Arts (EA) 95
electronic information industry, Chinese **17**
Eleventh Five-Year Plan 16
eLong 48, 53
e-mail service of Tencent 46
Epic Games 95
Expedia 48

Fab 77
Facebook 40, 92, 111
Feiliao 92
Fetion QQ 91, 93
first-person shooting (FPS) games 86–87
Five-Year Plans 14–16, 18
foreign direct investment (FDI) 21–2, 25
Foxmail 46
Fuchs, Christian 2, 113

game programs of Tencent 42–3, 94–6; *see also specific name*
Glu Mobile 96
Golden projects 13, 109
Goldman Sachs 35–6, 71, 112
Google 2, 110–11
GoPets Ltd. 95
GSM technology 91

haoma.com 89
Harvey, David 3
HBO 41–2
Hong Kong Stock Exchange (HKSE) 35, 67
Hong, Yu 4, 22
horizontal integration 45–8, 108
Hotmail 46
Huayi Brothers Media Corp. 51–2, 76

IBM 85
information and communication technology (ICT): BRICS and 111–12; capitalist expansion and, global 113; in China 1, 4–5, 10; crisis and, potential 113; industry 1, 111–12; PEC scholars and 2; venture capitalists and 112–13; wealth of 1
Informatization Office (State Council) 16
initial public offering (IPO) 20, 23–4, 36, 67
instant messaging (IM) service of Tencent 23, 33–4, 84–5; *see also* QQ.com
Institute of High Energy Physics 9
International Data Group (IDG) 65–6, 109, 112
Internet: China and 4, 9, 33–4; China's burgeoning companies involving 110; companies' emergence of (1995–2000) 20–1, **21**; "golden rule" of 64; mainstream studies of 2–3; political economy and, global 1–3; Tencent and history of in China 108–9; value-added services and 20; *see also* network infrastructure, building Chinese; Tencent; value-added services (VAS)
Internet Plus 19, 51–3, 109
Internet service providers (ISPs) 34
Internet value-added services (IVAS) of Tencent 36, 38, *38*

Jingdong (JD.com) 43, 47, 53
Joymax Development Ltd. 46
JPMorgan Chase and Co. 68–9

Kaixin001 76
Keyword Technology Ltd. 34
Kik 77
Kingsoft Internet Security Software Corp. Ltd. (KIS) 48
Kuaidi Dache 49
KuGou 88
Kuwo 88

labor practices of Tencent 44–5
Lau Chi Ping Martin 47, 71
League of Legends game 87, 95–6
Leju Holdings Ltd. 50
Level Up! International Holdings Limited 75–6, 95
Li Keqiang 19
Li, Minqi 4
Linchuan Qiu, Jack 23
Lin Chun 3
Lin Jun 63–4
logistics service of Tencent 49

Ma Chenshu 62–3
Ma Huateng 23, 33, 62–4, 69
Ma, Jack 20, 52, 68
Ma, Jian-nan 63
Ma, Steven 96
market reforms in China 18
massive multiplayer online games (MMOGs) 86, 94; *see also* online games of Tencent; *specific name*
massive online battle arena (MOBA) 95–6; *see also* online games of Tencent; *specific name*
McChesney, Robert 2–3
Media Asia Group Holdings Ltd. 52
media/film industry of Tencent 51–2
media platform of Tencent 41–2
Ministry of Culture (MOC) 63, 86
Ministry of Education 63
Ministry of Electronics Industry (MEI) 14, 16
Ministry of Industry and Information Technology (MITI) 15, 92–3
Ministry of Information Industry (MII) 16
Ministry of Posts and Telecommunications (MPT) 12–13, 16
Mirabilis (Israeli company) 33
Mobile QQ 91, 93
mobile and telecommunications value-added services (MVAS) of Tencent 36, 38, *38*, 46
mobile voice over Internet protocol (mVoIP) 92
Mosco, Vincent 1–2, 40
MSN e-mail 46
Muller, Milton 9
MultiChoice Africa Ltd. 68
Musk, Elon 77
Myriad International Holdings (MIH) 66–7, 74–5, 109

Nanjing Wangdian Technology Co. Ltd. 46
Naspers: Changsha and 74; expansion of 66–7; political economy profile of 71–2, *72*, *73*, 74–6; revenue by Internet segment (2018) *73*; revenue by region (2018) *73*; revenue by segment (2018) 72, *72*; Tencent and 62, 74–6, 109; Xin'an Media Co. Ltd. and 74
National Basketball Association (NBA) 41–2
National Bureau of Statistics (China) 20
National Development and Reform Commission (NDRC) 16, 92
National Information Work Leading Group (State Council) 15
National People's Congress 14, 18
National Science Foundation (China) 12
NavInfo Co. Ltd. 50
neoliberalism 3
Neowitz 86–7, 94
NetEase 20
Netmarble Games Corp. (formerly CJ Games Corp.) 96
network infrastructure, building Chinese: Internet as industrialization (1996–2010) 13–16; Internet as infrastructure (1994 and 1995) 12–13; Internet as pillar industry (2011–present) 18–19; overview 10–11; preparation (1987–1993) 11–12
Nextplay 94
Ninth Five-Year Plan (1996–2000) 14–16

OICQ 33–34
OkBuy 43

online advertising of Tencent 36, 42
online community of Tencent 46
online games of Tencent 42–3, 86–7, 94–6; *see also specific name*
online music of Tencent 88
online payment of Tencent 43, 48–9, 100
online publication/reading service of Tencent 87
online real estate service of Tencent 50
online review platform of Tencent 49
online software security of Tencent 48
online streaming platforms 92
online streaming portal of Tencent 41–2
online taxi reservation app of Tenent 48–9
online travel agency of Tencent 48
Outspark 100
over-the-top (OTT) content providers 92
ownership of Tencent 67–9, *68*, **69**, **70**, 71, 77–8

Paipai.com 43
PCCW 65–6, 109
Peking University 44
Peking University network (PUNET) 12
Pengyou.com 41
Ping An Insurance (Group) Co. 36
PlayerUnknown's Battlegrounds (PUBG) game 95
political economy of communication (PEC) 2
political economy, global: China and 1, 9–10, 24–5; critical 1–2; of Internet 1–3; Tencent and 108
political-economy theory of Internet: context of Tencent within history of Internet in China 108–9; financialization and 6, 111–13; integrated Tencent and 110; Internet as site to (re)conceptualize state-capital relations and 111; transnationalization and 6, 111–13; transnational Tencent and 109–10; *see also* Tencent
Ponysoft 63
Practo 77
PT Global Mediacom 100
*Punch Monster*game 94

Qihoo 360 47–8, 91
QQ.com: accounts (2004–18) **84**; birth of 23, 34; brand 88–9; building community of 88–90; as cultural product 83–4; international version of 100; JD.com and 43; monthly active users of 23; news reporting on 41; promoting 88–91; success of 40, 66, 84, 90, 111
QQ Game Portal 86
QQ Huaxia game 86
QQ Membership Club 89–90
QQ Music 88
QQ SanGuo game 86
QZone 40–1, 94

R2Bear game 94
real-name social-networking site (SNS) 41
Real Time eXchange (RTX) 85
Report on the Work of the Government (2015) 19
research and development of Tencent 43–4, **44**
ridesharing app of Tencent 48–9
Riot Games 87, 96
Roco Kingdom game 87
Roux, Antonie Andries 67, 71, 74

Sanook.com 75
Schiller, Dan 2, 111
Schiller, Herbert 2
search engine of Tencent 42, 46–7
Searle, Charles St. Leger 66–7, 74
Sephiroth game 86, 94
Sequoia Capital 112
Shambaugh, David 4
Shanda Cloudary 87
Shanghai World Exposition 41
shareholders of Tencent, major (2004–18) **69**
shareholding structure of Tencent after IPO 68, *68*
Shenzhen (China) 22, 24, 63–4
Shenzhen Baiyeyuan Investment Co. Ltd. 51
Shenzhen Domain Computer Network Co. Ltd. 86
Shenzhen Electronics Group 65
Shenzhen Li Ye Group Co. Ltd. 51
Shenzhen Shiji Kaixuan Technology Co. Ltd. 35

Shenzhen Telecome 65
Shenzhen WeBank Ltd. 51
Shidai Zhaoyang Technology Co. Ltd. 35
ShinJoung Yeo 2
Sichuan earthquake 41
Sina Weibo 47–48, 66
SMS 92–3
Smythe, Dallas 2
Snapchat 77
So, Alvin Y. 3
socialism, Chinese crisis of 3
social-networking site (SNS) 40–1
social platforms of Tencent 40–1
SoftBank 96
Sogou.com 42, 46–7, 53
Sohu.com 20
Soso.com 42
special economic zones (SEZs) 21–2, 63
SportsCn 74
State Development Planning Commission 12
State Economic Informatization Joint Meeting 15
State Education Commission (China) 12, 14
Supercell 87, 96

Tan, Zixiang 9 telecom industry, Chinese **17**
Tencent Collaboration Fund 76
Tencent Holdings Limited 68
Tencent Literature 87
Tencent Music Entertainment (TME) 88
Tencent Scholarship for Excellence in Science and Technology 44
Tencent Technology (Shenzhen) Co. Ltd. 34
Tenth Five-Year Plan 16
Tesla 77
Titan Media 74
trade services of Tencent 49
transnational expansion of Tencent 75, 97–101, 109–10
transnationalization and political-economy theory of Internet 6, 111–13
Tse, Edward 20
Tsinghua University network (TUNET) 12
Twelfth Five-Year Plan 18
21cn.com 65
Twitter 92

United Broadcasting Public Company Limited (UBC) 68
urban development in China 19–23

value-added services (VAS) 20, 23, 33–4, 42, 85, 91, 109; *see also specific type*
venture capitalists (VCs) 65, 77, 112–13
vertical integration 45, 48–51, 53, 83, 94–6, 108
Vertigo Games 94
Vnet Messenger (VIM) 91

Wallerstein, David A.M. 66, 76
Wang Zhongjun 52
Wang Zhonglei 52
Warface game 94
War of the Zombie game 94
Webzen 94
WeFire 96
Wei, Wu 9
Weixin/WeChat: Alibaba and 47; cultural profile of Tencent and 85, 91–3; debate on 91–3; development of 40; Didi Dache and 48–9; Internet Plus and 53; JD.com and 43; launching of 38, 85; micromarketing strategies of 32, 111; monthly active users **85**; online payment services of 48–9, 100; success of 111; Zhang Xiaolong and 46
Wen Jiabao 92
wireless application protocol (WAP) 34
wireless local loop (WILL) technology 91
World Cups 41
Wu Bangguo 15, 49
Wu Xiaobo 64
Wu, Xiaoguang 48

Xiaoyou.com 41
Xi Jinping 15–16, 19
Xin'an Media Co. Ltd. 74
Xu Chenye 23, 33, 63

Ying HaiWei 20
Yixun.com 43
YouTube 40

Zeitlin, Maurice 69
Zeng Liqing 23, 33
Zhang, Charles 20
Zhang Xiaolong 46
Zhang Yuzhou 63–4
Zhang Zhidon 23, 33, 63, 68–9, 71
Zhao, Yuezhi 4
Zhong Wang 20
Zhu Rongji 13, 15
Zou Jiahua 15
Zynga 94

For Product Safety Concerns and Information please contact our EU
representative GPSR@taylorandfrancis.com
Taylor & Francis Verlag GmbH, Kaufingerstraße 24, 80331 München, Germany

www.ingramcontent.com/pod-product-compliance
Ingram Content Group UK Ltd.
Pitfield, Milton Keynes, MK11 3LW, UK
UKHW020942210926
475569UK00020B/9
9780367195083